Quarterly Essay

1 MINORITY REPORT
The New Shape of Australian Politics
George Megalogenis

73 CORRESPONDENCE
Thomas Keneally, Emma Shortis, David Smith, Bruce Wolpe, Paul Kane, Don Watson

101 Contributors

Quarterly Essay is published four times a year by Black Inc., an imprint of Schwartz Books Pty Ltd. Publisher: Morry Schwartz.

ISBN 9781760644413 ISSN 1444-884x

Subscriptions – 1 year print & digital (4 issues): $99.99 within Australia incl. GST. Outside Australia $134.99. 1 year digital only: $64.99.

Payment may be made by Mastercard or Visa, or by cheque made out to Schwartz Books. Payment includes postage and handling.

To subscribe, fill out and post the subscription card or form inside this issue, or subscribe online:

quarterlyessay.com
subscribe@quarterlyessay.com
Phone: 61 3 9486 0288

Correspondence should be addressed to:

The Editor, Quarterly Essay
22–24 Northumberland Street
Collingwood VIC 3066 Australia
Phone: 61 3 9486 0288 / Fax: 61 3 9011 6106
Email: quarterlyessay@blackincbooks.com

Editor: Chris Feik. Management: Elisabeth Young. Publicity: Anna Lensky. Design: Guy Mirabella. Associate Editor: Kirstie Innes-Will. Production Coordinator: Marilyn de Castro. Typesetting: Typography Studio.

Printed in Australia by McPherson's Printing Group. The paper used to produce this book comes from wood grown in sustainable forests.

MINORITY REPORT

The New Shape of Australian Politics

George Megalogenis

The sword of minority government hangs over the major parties. It has threatened their viability ever since the shock of the 2010 federal election, when the Australian people cut down a first-term Labor government but stopped short of returning the Coalition to office.

Neither side commands an electoral base broad enough in the twenty-first century to guarantee that power, once secured, can be sustained for more than a single three-year term. That recognition had destabilised our democracy in the decade just past, as Labor and Coalition governments sacrificed four prime ministers between them to appease the impatient gods of opinion polling. Although the major parties are determined not to repeat that cycle of self-harm, the problem of their electoral relevance remains unanswered. Now the question turns to whether a return to minority government will further damage our democracy or, perhaps, revitalise it.

"Politics," John Howard was fond of saying, "is governed by the iron laws of arithmetic." It is also subject to the laws of irony. Today, Labor and the Coalition would kill for the support they received in 2010. That was the last campaign run on the old 40–40–20 rule, whereby the duopoly typically garnered at least 80 per cent of first-preference votes between them. Back then, the major parties convinced themselves that the protest vote had peaked and regular programming would soon resume. The theory, explained to me by MPs and advisers on both sides, was that the ordeal of Julia Gillard's minority government would act as an automatic stabiliser for the two-party system. Voters would not want to go there again.

But support for minor parties and independents continued to ratchet up in each subsequent campaign and reached an inevitable tipping point at the 2022 election, when the primary vote divided into a third each for Labor, the Coalition and none of the above. Another collective swing away from the major parties at the next election would make the none-of-the-above vote the largest bloc of the three.

This is a crucial distinction for Anthony Albanese's Labor government as it confronts the prospect of history repeating with the loss of its majority after a single term. The last hung parliament reflected a polarised electorate, split between Labor's majorities in the cosmopolitan south-east and the smaller states, and the Coalition's majorities in the frontier states of Queensland and Western Australia. The crossbench was drawn from the patriarchy. All five were men, three of whom were former National Party MPs. Only one, the Greens' first lower-house MP, Adam Bandt, represented a big-city electorate.

The next hung parliament, whenever it occurs and whoever leads it, will reflect a more fractured electorate, with new fault-lines opening within the cities which overlap the old rifts of identity between city and country, between women and men, and between young and old. The crossbench is three times larger, seating sixteen MPs at the last election. It skews towards urban Australia and is dominated by professional women who have had a life before politics. A parliament that looks more like the people it serves carries the promise of new ideas to test an economic model that has outlived its usefulness and a social model that still falls short of our egalitarian ideal. But it also risks forming into a new gridlock if the major parties and crossbench are in direct competition for seats – namely, Labor versus Green, and Liberal versus teal.

I should declare that I had some sympathy for the view in 2010 that Australia would be better served by stable majority government. One of the reasons was the narrowness of the all-male crossbench. But my main concern was the incentive that minority government provided for Oppositions to make Australia ungovernable, and for my profession, the media, to fixate on opinion polls. Now I am not so sure. A volatile minority government may be the lesser evil when compared to the narrowly cast and ineffectual governments of the past decade.

Then again, the combinations of parties and personalities that can make a hung parliament unworkable are seemingly endless. Is this what the Australian people intended when they broke the two-party system at the last election? It's a trick question, because the none-of-the-above vote in 2022 bore little resemblance to the electoral shocks of Brexit and Trump. Our protest vote was directed at both major parties at once, with an epicentre in the cities, not regional and rural electorates, the traditional home of political cynicism.

Ten seats in total moved from the major parties to the crossbench at the 2022 election – six from the Liberals to teal candidates across Sydney, Melbourne and Perth; two from the Liberal National Party to the Greens in Brisbane, while Labor lost a heartland seat in western Sydney to an independent and a Brisbane-based seat to the Greens.

A comparison with Britain's July 2024 election shows the Australian difference. The British people followed our lead by electing a Labour government with just a third of the primary vote, and sent a record number of women to the House of Commons (40.5 per cent, compared to the 39.1 per cent elected to our House of Representatives in 2022). The UK's voluntary first-past-the-post voting system secured a landslide victory for Keir Starmer's Labour; under our compulsory preferential voting system, Albanese's Labor squeaked in with a majority of two seats.

The revelation is in the splintering of the conservative vote. The majority of those who turned against Scott Morrison's blokey government created a new independent female centre in the cities; by contrast, in the UK the Tories lost ground to the nationalist right. Where former Liberal voters elected Zoe Daniel and Allegra Spender to the House of Representatives, their counterparts in the UK sent Brexit town crier and Donald Trump supporter Nigel Farage to the House of Commons.

Australia's protest vote sits in a global category of its own at the moment because it aims to force change on the system, not disrupt it. This tells us something about our underlying trust in the idea of government, and our willingness to be led from the centre, not the fringe. Whether it achieves its ambition will depend on the long-term significance of the last election. Did it signal a realignment which transferred power from the conservative regions to the progressive cities? Or was it just another version of the stalemate we have endured since 2010, in which no major party is able to govern with authority because each represents only a fraction of a divided nation?

I have framed this essay as a stocktake and a preview of the next election. Did voters get what they wanted in 2022? And if not, whom will they punish for it? The stocktake will cover the major and minor parties and provide a guide to what success or failure would look like for each. While I will avoid making forecasts, I trust you will find the tools to interpret the result of the next election within these pages. I will treat this forty-seventh parliament as a dry run for the next hung parliament, and use the case studies of the Voice referendum and the housing affordability crisis to test the capacity of a multi-party system to deliver reform.

I am mindful that one campaign's gravitational pull can be irrelevant by the time of the next contest. No one watching Anthony Albanese claim victory on 21 May 2022 and committing his government to implementing the Uluru Statement from the Heart "in full" could have foreseen the collapse of Labor's progressive constituency just eighteen months later.

Labor had made history less than twelve months into its term by becoming the first government in more than a century to claim a seat from the Opposition at a by-election. That seat, Aston, in Melbourne's outer east, represented Peter Dutton's preferred suburban battleground. Albanese did not see the swing coming on April Fool's Day 2023, so he was not even in Melbourne to join the Labor candidate, Mary Doyle, as she claimed victory.

Dutton accepted responsibility for the loss, but then placed a double-or-nothing bet on dividing the country. He announced that the Liberal Party would campaign against the Aboriginal and Torres Strait Islander Voice to Parliament, the centrepiece of the Uluru Statement from the Heart.

Referendums to change the Australian constitution are notoriously difficult to pass. Only one has achieved the required double majority of voters and states without bipartisan support: the Chifley Labor government's 1946 referendum on social services. The Voice was doomed from the moment Dutton took up the "No" case, based on research from the Australia National University. Support for the Voice was at 60 per cent in April 2023 and had fallen below 50 per cent by August. The verdict on 14 October was a resounding "No": 60.1 per cent to 39.9 per cent. All six states rejected the Voice, with the "Yes" vote ranging from a high of 45.9 per cent in Victoria to a low of 31.8 per cent in Dutton's Queensland.

The ANU concluded that "it was the large decline in the Coalition vote that led to the referendum not passing, rather than the smaller decline amongst Labor voters."

The referendum reshuffled the electorate back into the familiar patterns of the Howard era, with the regions and outer suburbs united behind the status quo and alienated from their fellow Australians in the cities, who cast a forlorn ballot for change. It was a victory for gridlock, which demonstrated the residual power of a major party to stop things, even as the Liberals faced serious questions of identity of their own following the loss of former blue-ribbon seats to the teals and Greens.

I've taken the Voice as the starting point from which to compose a report card for our first post-duopoly parliament, and to correct for the silence that followed the referendum. Did the "No" vote of 2023 cancel the progressive protest vote of 2022, and what does it tell us about the next election?

SPLITTING THE INNER CITY FROM THE SUBURBS

The private discussions between Anthony Albanese and Peter Dutton in early 2023, when a bipartisan agreement on the Voice remained on the table, would veer from the big picture of reconciliation to a subconscious exchange of notes on the next federal election. The prime minister wanted the leader of the Opposition to appreciate the political cost of campaigning for a "No" vote. The eight electorates that switched from the Liberals to the teals across Sydney, Melbourne and Perth, and from the Liberal National Party to the Greens in Brisbane in 2022, were almost certain to vote "Yes" and would not forgive Dutton if the referendum failed. The same theory applied to Tony Abbott's old seat of Warringah, on Sydney's northern beaches, which fell to independent Zali Steggall in 2019 and swung further away from the Liberals in 2022. Take all nine off the tally board, and the Coalition would have to find seats in Labor areas where it had never won before if it was to form majority government again.

The rub, as Albanese put it, was that those who voted "No" won't necessarily mark their ballot paper for the Liberal or National parties at the next election. "No" would move on but "Yes" wouldn't forget: that was the summary of what the prime minister told his opponent.

Albanese's gratuitous advice was delivered from a position of assumed strength. The new Labor government was still in its honeymoon phase, and every poll taken to that point had the referendum on course for success. When Indigenous campaigners for the Voice urged him to consider offering Dutton a form of co-authorship, perhaps by making him chair of the committee to design the model after the referendum, Albanese suggested that he did not need the Liberals to win. He reminded people that the electorate broke 40–30–30 against the major parties. "We are no longer 40–40–20," he explained.

While Albanese imagined an openhearted majority, Dutton realised that the Voice could not pass without his support. He had the referendum precedent of 1999 to guide him, when an unholy alliance of Coalition supporters beyond the inner city and Labor's traditional base in the suburbs defeated the proposal for a republic. In particular, he had his eye on the blood-red corner of the federal electoral map which Scott Morrison had targeted without success in 2022: western Sydney.

Western Sydney is burdened by clichés coined in the Howard era which have little relevance to the place or its people. "Howard's battlers" and their twenty-first-century iteration, "Tony's tradies," are consciously white labels which better fit the voters who reside on the outskirts of Sydney. They represent an idea of Old Australia which successive Liberal leaders have defended against the straw men of migration from Asia and the Middle East.

In reality, western Sydney is the nation's most diverse urban area, with a concentration of New Australians that is about a decade ahead of Melbourne's most diverse suburbs to the north and west, and two decades ahead of Brisbane's west. A string of suburbs – from Parramatta at its northern edge to Bankstown in the south and to Fairfield in its middle west – have between 85 and 90 per cent of residents born overseas or with at least one migrant parent. The Sydney-wide average, by comparison, is 67 per cent; the national figure is 51 per cent. Plainly, this is not the natural home of the party of Howard, Abbott, Morrison or Dutton.

Yet western Sydney fascinates the Liberals because it happens to be the most socially conservative urban area in Australia. The evidence is in previous referendums. Western Sydney uniquely rejected both the republic in 1999 and same-sex marriage in 2017.

To a binary political mind like Dutton's, the Voice presented the opportunity for a third "No" vote against change, to remind Labor's migrant working-class base of the distance between them and the inner-city trendies. If the previously safe Liberal seats in the big four cities, which are wealthier and better-educated than the nation at large, can turn to the teals and Greens, why wouldn't Labor's own urban heartland – the seats in Sydney and Melbourne which are more diverse and more religious – embrace conservative independents or even Liberal candidates in future?

Provoking a culture war on the Labor side was not Dutton's primary motivation for killing the Voice. Maintaining Coalition unity was a much higher priority. Dutton believed that his colleagues would turn on each other if he called for a "Yes" vote. The alternative of a free vote, which the monarchist John Howard had allowed the Liberals in 1999, was impractical for the same reason. Why risk a schism over Labor's agenda?

Dutton's approach was shaped by the memory of his previous time in Opposition, when the Coalition was negotiating a deal with Kevin Rudd's Labor government to introduce an emissions trading scheme. The issue split the Liberal and National parties, and the Liberals burned through three leaders between 2007 and 2009 before setting a final course for obstruction. That hard "No" under Abbott restored a sense of purpose to the Opposition and triggered government panic as the polls tightened. It has informed Dutton's approach to every difficult issue, from the Middle East to housing affordability: take an uncompromising position to the right to make the government look weak and indecisive.

Albanese underestimated how the balance of power within the Coalition itself would encourage Dutton to run an aggressive campaign against the Voice. The fallout from the 2022 election had left the Coalition with a disproportionate share of regional seats in the House of Representatives, and reduced the Liberals outside Queensland to a minority faction for the first time in the party's history. This meant the Opposition was overrepresented by MPs whose electorates were most likely to be hostile to the Voice. Bipartisanship would place those MPs in direct conflict with independents to their right, including the protest parties of Pauline Hanson and Clive Palmer.

The Nationals had already declared their opposition to the Voice in November 2022, before they had even seen a draft question. Andrew Gee, a former minister in the Morrison government, quit the party in protest and moved to the crossbench. His NSW electorate of Calare had previously been held by popular local independent Peter Andren during the Howard era.

NSW Liberal senator Andrew Bragg said Gee's defection made a conscience vote imperative for the Liberals. Bragg said the referendum was "not about the politicians, it's about the public having their say."

When Aston fell to the Albanese government at the by-election in April 2023, the numbers in the House of Representatives stood at Labor seventy-eight, the Coalition fifty-six, and seventeen on the crossbench. The Coalition's share of the parliament was now at its lowest point in eighty years. Dutton's strategy of reclaiming government from the suburbs looked like wishful thinking. Yet he chose this very moment to join with the Nationals against the Voice, to give the Coalition something to fight for.

The response from the moderate wing of the Liberal Party was swift but ultimately ineffectual. Ken Wyatt, the former Indigenous Affairs minister in the Morrison government, resigned from the party within twenty-four hours of the announcement. Dutton's Indigenous Australians spokesperson, Julian Leeser, quit his portfolio days later so he could campaign for the Voice as a backbencher. The Tasmanian premier, Jeremy Rockliff, the last Liberal standing at the time after the defeat of the NSW Coalition government of Dominic Perrottet, restated his support for the referendum. Rockliff's predecessor, Peter Gutwein, accused Dutton and his team of "attempting to confuse the Australian people." He said "straw-man arguments" against the Voice "will do nothing to advance the cause of First Nations people in this country."

But these criticisms did not deter Dutton. He appointed Northern Territory senator Jacinta Nampijinpa Price, a self-described Warlpiri-Celtic woman opposed to the Voice and who sat with the Nationals, not the Liberals, in Leeser's place. Those Liberals who had been calling for a free vote, in keeping with the Menzies tradition, quietly fell into line behind the "No" campaign.

*

Anthony Albanese assumed he was pushing on an open door with the Voice, with the path laid out for him by the realignment of the electorate the year before. The 2022 campaign was the first in our history to be decided in the capital cities alone, and it broke, for Labor, the spell that Queensland had held over the political system since the 1990s. To Albanese's mind, the more Peter Dutton looked at the rest of Australia through the blinkers of Queensland parochialism, the better it would be for Labor because the Liberals would remain locked out of the capitals.

Our two most populous cities, Melbourne and Sydney, are the keys to both the realignment and the collapse of the Voice. It's worth taking a step back to understand what I mean by realignment before exploring the meaning of the referendum's failure.

I have revisited every federal election since Robert Menzies led the modern Liberal Party into power in 1949 to identify when the political centre shifted from one era to the next. Which city or state was most likely to deliver a majority of seats to the winning party at a federal election?

The short answer is that the centre swapped states every two decades, as economic power and population moved from south to north.

Middle-class and protected Victoria picked the winner across all nine elections held between 1949 and 1969, when it was regarded as the jewel in the Liberal crown. The baton passed to the free-trader New South Wales in the ten elections between 1972 and 1993, when Labor governments dominated the reform era; and to the people magnet of Queensland during the Howard era, when our whitest and most decentralised mainland state sided with the victor in eight of the nine elections held between 1996 and 2019. Victoria, the most urban of the three states, saw its influence decline with each changing of the centre. Its people predicted eight of the ten elections during the NSW phase, and just three of the nine during the Queensland phase.

Australia's post-war development is mirrored in these changes. Victoria's primacy during the full employment decades of the 1950s and '60s reflected its position as the nation's manufacturing base. The political centre transferred to New South Wales as financial power shifted from Melbourne to Sydney in the 1970s and '80s, and the economy was disrupted by three deep recessions. Queensland replaced its southern neighbour through its natural advantages of internal migration and resources.

The 2022 election cut Queensland out of the equation for the first time since 1984, and tilted the electoral playing field back towards Melbourne and Sydney. Consider what the next parliament would look like if the Liberals reclaimed the four seats they lost to Labor in Perth and returned Western Australia to the conservative column alongside Queensland. Now let's assume that no Coalition seats are lost anywhere else in the country. Dutton would still be sixteen seats short of a majority. This is why Melbourne and Sydney will most likely determine who forms the next government, whether majority or minority. The Liberals hold just eight of the forty-five seats to be contested across the two capitals, against thirty for Labor and seven on the crossbench. Dutton is unlikely to be prime minister while the Victorian and NSW capitals are voting Labor, teal and Green.

Melbourne and Sydney represent the fourth phase of Australia's post-war development – migration-led growth from India and China. This is the economic and cultural story behind the realignment to a new joint centre. Between them, Melbourne and Sydney are home to 40 per cent of the Australian people and more than half of all Australians born overseas. But they have received more than 60 per cent of the migrants from India, and more than 70 per cent of those from China and Vietnam.

The overseas migration program has been the dominant driver of our population growth since the final years of the Howard government. The statistic that warrants closer attention for all sides of politics is the growth in the second-generation population – the local-born children of migrants. Their numbers increased by almost 1.2 million between the 2011 and 2021 census. That was double the number added to the Old Australian population – those who have parents and grandparents born here. Just over half of these 1.2 million people were born in Sydney and Melbourne.

Our political system was whiter and more masculine than the national average while Queensland was the swing state. Now it is being forced to engage with the people of Melbourne and Sydney on their terms as New Australians.

*

Peter Dutton should be able to recite the admonition he received from the Liberal Party's post-mortem into the 2022 campaign. Dutton was not directly named, nor was the former prime minister Scott Morrison. But they bore joint responsibility for alienating the Chinese Australian community in the lead-up to the last election. Dutton, in his role as Home Affairs Minister and then Defence Minister, was arguably more belligerent than Morrison. His warning early in the campaign that Australia should "prepare for war" with China was particularly unhelpful in Melbourne's inner south-east and east and Sydney's harbourside electorates.

"The swing against the Liberal Party was significantly greater in electorates which have a higher concentration of voters of Chinese ancestry," the review found. "In the top 15 seats by Chinese ancestry the swing against the Party (on a 2PP basis) was 6.6%, compared to 3.7% in other seats. There were a number of reasons for this, including a perception the previous Government's criticisms of the CCP [Chinese Communist Party] government of China included the wider Chinese community more generally."

The number the review wanted drilled into every Liberal MP, adviser, party official and volunteer was 1.4 million: the number of Australians who recorded Chinese ancestry at the 2021 census. Chinese Australians represent 5.5 per cent of the nation's population, compared to 3 per cent twenty years earlier, the review noted. "Rebuilding the Party's relationship with the Chinese community must therefore be a priority during this term of Parliament."

Rebuilding that relationship through a "No" campaign did not seem to make short-term political sense, based on the initial polling. Research conducted for the Uluru Dialogue in April 2023, after Dutton announced his opposition to the Voice, found that seven in ten Asian migrants and their local-born children were in favour of it. Only Aboriginal and Torres Strait Islanders recorded a higher level of support.

The first of the ANU surveys, in January 2023, also found that 74 per cent of people who spoke a language other than English at home intended to vote "Yes", compared to 56 per cent of those who spoke English only. The

New Australian vote for the Voice held up through the winter of 2023, even as the national vote slipped below 50 per cent. The migrant swing came very late in the campaign, over the course of September and October, and it was responsible for pulling the overall vote below 40 per cent. The ANU exit poll found that 39.5 per cent of non-English speakers and 35.6 per cent English-only speakers voted "No" at the referendum.

The ANU concluded with a certain academic understatement: "It would seem that the yes campaign struggled to reach non-English speakers."

Dutton and the "No" campaign managed to unite New and Old Australians against First Australians in the final stage of referendum, when the Voice was already lost. But the tactical victory came at the risk of reinforcing the view within New Australia, and especially in Melbourne and Sydney, that the Liberals are the party of the race card.

*

The Voice answered a question that wasn't on the ballot paper, about the divides of identity and class between the capitals, regional cities and the bush. Only three capitals and two regional cities returned a majority "Yes" vote in 2023: Melbourne, Canberra, Hobart, Newcastle and Wollongong. This marked a substantial narrowing of the progressive constituency that was revealed in the republic referendum in 1999, when every capital except Perth voted "Yes," as did Newcastle and Wollongong.

The story of Sydney's transformation from "Yes" to "No" is fascinating because of what it says about Anthony Albanese's sway in his hometown. Nine of the city's twenty-five electorates voted for the Voice. In 1999, the score in favour of the republic was twelve seats to ten when Prime Minister John Howard was urging a "No" vote.

Sydney's deepening culture rift is best seen by rail, on the forty-six-minute journey from Wynyard Station in the CBD to Bankstown in the heart of the western suburbs. The train line winds through four safe Labor seats, represented by the prime minister and three senior cabinet ministers: in order of travel, Tanya Plibersek's Sydney, Albanese's Grayndler, Tony Burke's

Watson and Jason Clare's Blaxland. The "Yes" vote dissolves as you leave the inner south and turn due west at Marrickville, from 79.4 per cent at Grayndler to 42.1 per cent at Watson and 38.3 per cent at Blaxland.

These splits had been foreshadowed by the marriage equality plebiscite six years earlier. Only seventeen of the nation's 151 electorates voted "No" in 2017. Twelve were in western Sydney. Blaxland returned the nation's lowest "Yes" vote of 26.1 per cent; inner-city Sydney and Melbourne recorded the equal highest – 83.7 per cent – in a referendum that was passed by all six states and with a national vote of 61.6 per cent.

Anthony Albanese tells me that the misinformation campaign against the Voice struck a particular nerve in Sydney's migrant suburbs. He cites the feedback from the Addi Road Community Centre in Marrickville, in the heart of Grayndler. Regarded as the birthplace of multiculturalism in the 1970s, the organisation ran a series of community programs during the referendum. Migrant supporters of the Voice brought in pamphlets written in their own languages that had been placed in local letterboxes. They pushed a range of conspiracy theories, from Indigenous students being granted preference at local independent schools to property claims being made against ordinary family homes.

These leaflets, Albanese tells me, were designed to tell New Australians that "First Nations people would be granted special rights above them."

"So many, many people were worried that this would have a negative impact on their life, whereas the reality is it would have had an impact on the life of First Nations people but for most Australians it wouldn't have had a direct impact at all," he says.

When Peter Dutton allied the Liberals with the Nationals against the referendum, he gave the prime minister the option of delaying the vote. Albanese could have agreed that it was too hard to proceed without bipartisanship, and that he did not wish to subject Aboriginal and Torres Strait Islanders to the heartbreak of a vote that was now likely to be "No." But he never took the call seriously. He weighed the history of referendums that had failed without bipartisan support against the range of organisations that were lined up for the "Yes" campaign, and assumed their combined influence would prevail.

"There was substantial support for the Voice from the other side of politics," Albanese explains. He included on that list Tony Nutt, the former Liberal Party federal director and chief of staff to John Howard, and Mark Textor, the former Liberal Party pollster, as well as current and former Liberal premiers. Every major sporting organisation supported the Voice, along with business and community groups. "But nothing could overcome the lack of bipartisanship," he concedes.

The political opposition to the Voice became a self-fulfilling argument for the status quo, that inserting a confusing new power into the Constitution would do more harm than good. "[Their] simple campaign of 'If you are not absolutely certain, then vote No,' proved to be resounding," says Albanese.

He says that he and others in the "Yes" camp "underestimated" the power of social media to distort the debate. The volume of misinformation "about people losing their homes" fed into genuine concerns about the cost of living. Finally, he cites Noel Pearson's observation that most Australians do not interact with Indigenous Australians. "A combination of factors, of which the key one was the lack of bipartisanship."

The main driver of the "No" vote, according to the ANU exit poll, was the concern that the Voice would divide the country. "Amongst those that voted yes, the most important reason was that it would deliver better outcome[s] [for Aboriginal and Torres Strait Islander people]."

The survey included an "index of values" towards Aboriginal and Torres Islander people. It measured the attitudes of non-Indigenous Australians across a spectrum. "Higher values are related to a greater support for government intervention to support Aboriginal and Torres Strait Islander Australians, lower values are related to a belief that Aboriginal and Torres Islander Australians should be treated equally, and injustices are mostly in the past."

Women, younger Australians and Aboriginal and Torres Strait Islanders had a "higher values index," while non-English speaking migrants and those who had not completed Year 12 had a "lower values index." This reflects the emerging rift between socially progressive younger Australians and socially conservative New Australians.

Placing the social X-ray of the Voice over the previous votes for the republic and marriage equality reveals the double edge of a politics centred in Melbourne and Sydney. The inner cities are becoming more socially liberal as young professionals move in, while the migrant suburbs are becoming more socially conservative. This divide within the capitals is relatively new, especially in Melbourne, which has traditionally been a more cohesive city than Sydney. The Voice also widened the pre-existing gulf between the inner city and the bush, which was first exposed in the republic referendum.

In 2023, as in 1999, the electorates of Melbourne and Maranoa, in the southern Queensland outback, returned the nation's highest and lowest "Yes" votes respectively. In Adam Bandt's Melbourne, support for the Voice was almost double the national vote: 77.2 per cent versus 39.9 per cent. In Maranoa, held by the Nationals' leader, David Littleproud, it was less than half: 15.4 per cent. The vote for the republic had been more evenly distributed: 70.2 per cent in Melbourne, 45.1 per cent nationally and 22.9 per cent in Maranoa.

The republic had enjoyed a discreet level of bipartisan support among Labor and Liberal voters in 1999, even though the then prime minister campaigned against it. Of the forty-two electorates that voted "Yes" in a parliament of 148, twenty-five were Labor and seventeen Liberal, including John Howard's own Bennelong and Tony Abbott's Warringah, two safe electorates with harbour views which are now in Labor and teal hands respectively.

The Voice claimed eight fewer "Yes" electorates than the republic: thirty-four in a parliament of 151. Of these thirty-four, twenty-one were Labor, twelve crossbench and just one Liberal. Mark this as a pyrrhic victory for Peter Dutton because the crossbench contingent included all nine seats that the Liberals had relinquished to the teals and Greens since 2019. By opposing the Voice, Dutton gifted the teals and Greens a midterm excuse to reboot their grassroots campaigns.

Let's quote once more from the Liberal Party's post-mortem of the 2022 campaign: "The Liberal Party is a national party which exists to form Government based on the widest possible support of the community. The Party must concede no seat and must vigorously contest the Teal seats at the next election … No party that is seeking to form Government has a pathway to a majority solely through rural and regional electorates."

The review acknowledged that Labor won a majority of the female vote across all age groups in 2022, and that in the teal seats the successful female candidates won a majority of the female vote. The Liberal vote was weakest among young women aged eighteen to thirty-four, and it is here that Dutton took his greatest risk in opposing the Voice because of the handicap he carries from the last election.

Inner metropolitan seats, which cover almost a third of the federal parliament, are becoming younger than the electorate at large due to the influx of local-born professionals and skilled migrants, who are more likely to be renters than home owners. The Liberals hold just four out of forty-five inner metropolitan seats at the moment and could lose another one or two at the next election, based on the results of the Voice.

As the ANU noted, "Younger Australians were more likely to vote yes than older Australians, with those aged 18 to 24 years at the time of the referendum more than twice as likely to vote yes as those aged 75 years and over (58.6 per cent compared to 24.2 per cent)."

The question for Dutton turns to whether the rejection of the Voice in the migrant suburbs cancels the progressive realignment of 2022. If the answer is yes, he can conceivably bring Labor down in a single term and form his own minority government without needing to regain inner metropolitan seats from Labor, teals and Greens. But that would rely on New Australians casting their first ever vote for the Liberals. A migrant "No" to the Voice is unlikely to be followed by a "Yes" if Dutton's next election campaign is based on a call to slash migration.

WASTING A PROGRESSIVE MANDATE

I have been looking forward to the rise of the New Australian voter. The concentration of migrants and their local-born children in the capitals, increasingly in election-deciding numbers, will reduce the threat of a Trump, Farage or Le Pen–style politics infecting our system. But a diverse electorate does not of itself guarantee a return to a more reform-minded politics for Australia. Our system is prone to inertia, and the habits of gridlock developed over the past decade and half could easily become entrenched if the parties divide by people and place. The risk is that the major and minor parties each take the path of least demographic resistance and create a parliament of competing identities, defined by location, age and education – young and Green in the CBD, teal and professional in the leafy suburbs, Labor in the migrant suburbs and gentrified provincial cities, Liberal on the whiter fringes of the cities and Nationals in the bush.

When I was digging through the past to establish the political centre by place, I was looking at a world in which the major parties viewed questions of identity as a contest to define Australia on behalf of the broadest possible national constituency, at a time when most of the population was from Old Australia – that is, white. The mortgage belt of the suburbs tethered Labor and Liberal to campaigning for the same swinging voter.

What the last election hinted at, and the referendum on the Voice clarified, is that the major parties have found themselves on opposite sides of the fault-line between New and Old Australia, and between city and country. Neither has the language at the moment to build a bridge between the two – a bridge that would, incidentally, secure stable majority government for the first party that inspires both constituencies.

The Voice offered a story that could bind both versions of Australia without recrimination. But it was beyond the skillset of Anthony Albanese to deliver on its promise, or the imagination of Peter Dutton to appreciate that a "Yes" vote might serve to keep Old Australia in the political centre. The shift in economic and electoral power to the Labor, teal and Green bases of

Melbourne, Sydney and even Brisbane – and the increasing diversity of those cities through skilled migration – will inevitably test social cohesion if the taxpayers of New Australia become estranged from the retirees and welfare recipients of Old Australia in rural and regional seats. This is the opposite challenge of nativism. Where the losers from globalisation have the numbers to continually disrupt the politics of the US, Britain and Europe, Australia's pendulum is swinging towards the voters living in the cosmopolitan centre, not outside it.

Both leaders bear responsibility for the souring of the national mood during the referendum. The failure of the Voice adds to the impression that Albanese is a poor campaigner. Voters forgave his stumbles in the last election because they were determined to dismiss the Morrison government. But will they cut him the same slack when he seeks a second term? Greater statesmen than Albanese – Menzies, Whitlam and Hawke – lost referendums without it costing them the next election. But they also saw their majority reduced when they faced the people for the first time as incumbent. Every incoming federal government of the post-war era went backwards on seeking re-election. Albanese has been witness to the past three examples as a member of parliament. The Howard government surrendered nineteen seats to Labor in 1998; the Gillard government lost eleven seats in net terms to the Coalition and crossbench in 2010; and the Turnbull government shed fourteen seats to Labor in 2016. The loss of just three seats would send Albanese's government into minority.

Albanese painted himself into a corner on the Voice. The referendum he committed to was a second-order issue for Australians. The ANU found that 61 per cent of voters "cared a good deal about the outcome." The comparable poll in 1999 found the care factor for the republic referendum was ten points higher, at 71 per cent. Knowing the electorate was disengaged, Albanese had to persuade them to share his ambition. That demanded a level of oratory beyond his halting, measured range, and a grassroots campaign beyond the capabilities of a major political party that counts only a third of the electorate as its base. Albanese wasted the political capital that every new prime minister is gifted on a lost cause. He could not even console himself with the electorate's regret once the consequences of the "No" vote had been absorbed. Because there was none.

Polling conducted almost a year after the referendum found no public appetite for parts two and three of the Uluru Statement from the Heart. Barely a third of voters supported beginning "work on a Treaty" or having a "Truth-Telling Commission to investigate historical and ongoing injustices committed against Aboriginal and Torres Strait Islander people." Even the soft conservative options of a legislated Voice or recognising "Aboriginal and Torres Strait Islander people in the constitution through another referendum, without establishing a Voice" (positions which Dutton has previously held) had the support of only one in three voters, with a slightly larger proportion opposed.

"Consistent feedback on the reasons for a no vote both before and after the referendum was that the Voice was divisive and would give First Nations people 'rights and privileges' that other Australians didn't enjoy," Peter Lewis, executive director of Essential, wrote in *The Guardian* in August 2024. "Think about that: we have lost so much faith in government to listen to us (rather than impose its will from on high) that simply being heard is perceived as a form of 'special treatment.'"

The idea for the Voice originated outside the political system. It was developed following the largest community consultation of its kind, across eight capitals and five regional centres. The Regional Dialogues on constitutional recognition rank alongside the campaign for female suffrage either side of Federation as a case study in grassroots democracy. But that consensus was picked apart by partisanship, as the old-school media of print and television deferred to Indigenous politicians over community leaders and constitutional experts. The prominence of Jacinta Nampijinpa Price and Victorian senator Lidia Thorpe suited Dutton's goal of reducing the referendum to an argument between political tribes: the populists versus the elites. Dutton characterised the Voice as a "Canberra-based bureaucracy" created for the benefit of Indigenous "academics" – including Professor Megan Davis, a co-author of the Uluru Statement from the Heart, and Professor Marcia Langton, a co-author of the report to the Morrison government on options for implementing the Voice. This repeated, perhaps without his realising it, one of the oldest colonial fallacies: that a "black" person can be made "white" by education and property. Once assimilated, they can't possibly speak for First Australians in remote communities or townships.

To be fair to Dutton, his disregard of Indigenous expertise is consistent with the approach of successive Liberal leaders to climate science. This is not to excuse his approach, but to place his reflex hostility to alternative views in political context. Dutton is a graduate of a system that privileges political power above all. He has only known a world in which the public service is easily cowed by ministers and their staff, and the media are too weak and divided to perform their basic duty of scrutiny.

Dutton entered parliament in 2001. John Howard perfected the politics of race in that year's election campaign by uniting Old and New Australia against asylum seekers who arrived by boat. Dutton characterised the Voice in the same disingenuous but potent way. First Australians were effectively jumping the queue to demand rights not available to anyone else.

But Dutton did not offer an alternative that would lift Indigenous Australians and bring the country together. This was beyond his range as the leader of the whitest and most masculine segment of the parliament. Nor did he seem all that interested in building a post-referendum bridge between the "No" voters of Old and New Australia. On the contrary, he took his tactical victory against the Voice as proof that he could bring down the government by creating a sense of identity crisis in the community, which casts Labor as the party of minority interests against a political centre he assumes is still majority white.

*

By grim coincidence, the final week of the referendum campaign was dominated by the external shock of Gaza. The Hamas attack on Israel on 7 October 2023, and Israel's scorched-earth retaliation, stirred the twin demons of Islamophobia and antisemitism in the Australian community and polarised the parliament.

I don't doubt that the political positions are genuinely held. But they are testing the very genius of our migration policies, which allow new arrivals and their local-born children to leave behind the disputes of the old country. That idea has its roots in the grand bargain of colonial settlement which gave rights to Irish Catholics on Australian soil that were not available at the time in the United Kingdom. It was revived after World War II with the successful settlement of former enemies from Germany and Poland, Italy and Greece.

The ASIO director-general, Mike Burgess, issued a prompt warning to community leaders after the Hamas attack not to inflame tensions. On 12 October, he said, "it is important that all parties consider the implications for social cohesion when making public statements. As I have said previously, words matter. ASIO has seen direct connections between inflamed language and inflamed community tensions."

As Phil Coorey reported in the *Australian Financial Review*:

> The statement was issued just hours after Labor was privately expressing outrage at an interview Opposition Leader Peter Dutton gave to 2GB radio host Ray Hadley.
>
> Asked whether he agreed "that part of the DNA of some Labor people is just to hate the Israelis," Mr Dutton replied: "I think there's certainly that element to it, Ray. I mean, there's a political element to it as well, because people like [Energy Minister] Chris Bowen, [Industry Minister] Ed Husic and others will be playing to their electorates."

The ASIO boss stepped up his warning a year later, addressing it to the parliament without naming any individual or party. "I get robust political debate, that's got to continue as a strong part of society but, just be careful with your language because, again, inflamed language leads to violence."

Dutton would not be silenced. He sensed Labor's vulnerability and had the precedent of Tony Abbott's relentless campaign on border protection during the Rudd/Gillard years to guide him. He accused Labor of not vetting the refugees it had already accepted from Gaza, and called for a ban on further arrivals. Again ASIO was drawn into the controversy – Dutton was suggesting that Labor had ordered ASIO to somehow skate around the security checks to determine if the applicant for a humanitarian visa was a supporter of Hamas. Burgess told Niki Savva he took strong exception "to those who keep distorting my words."

On the first anniversary of 7 October, Dutton refused to support a government-led motion which unequivocally condemned "Hamas's terror attacks on Israel" and called for the release of hostages, while it also mourned "the death of all innocent civilians" and called for a ceasefire. Dutton said the prime minister should "stand condemned" for "trying to speak out of both sides of his mouth." The parliament, he said, should show "respect to the Jewish community" without equivocation. The Greens abstained from the vote. Adam Bandt said his party could not support "a motion about a year of ongoing slaughter that fails to condemn the war crimes of the extremist Netanyahu government, acknowledge the unfolding genocide in Gaza, or put any pressure on Netanyahu's government to stop the invasions of Palestine and Lebanon."

Dutton and Bandt, with no lived experience as members of minority groups, or a thread of Jewish or Arab DNA between them, see no domestic risk in taking sides over the Middle East. I can only assume that they don't understand the fire they are playing with: how the Coalition's unconditional defence of Israel on the one hand, or the Greens' demand for immediate Palestinian statehood and sanctions against Israel on the other, can be taken by Arab, Muslim and Jewish Australians as a comment on their respective worth as people. Xenophobia's oldest card is the one of guilt by association: white Australia's insinuation that minority communities are somehow responsible for the crimes of individuals here, or for the actions of terrorist organisations overseas, or even for the policies of a foreign government. Mercifully, the Greens have not gone as far as former Liberal senator Eric Abetz, who demanded that Chinese Australians "unconditionally condemn the Chinese Communist Party dictatorship." Meanwhile, Aboriginal and Torres Strait Islanders will be wondering why the Greens didn't devote as much energy to the Voice as they have to Gaza. At least Jacinta Nampijinpa Price and Lidia Thorpe had skin in the referendum debate.

No federal government has the luxury of grandstanding in its conduct of foreign policy, especially in the Middle East, where Australia has little, if any, influence to begin with. Dutton, as a former Defence minister, would appreciate that Australia might be called on to provide troops for a peacekeeping force in the event of a ceasefire.

The late Martin Indyk, a former US ambassador to Israel, wrote earlier this year that Australia, along with Canada, India and South Korea, would tick the three necessary boxes for involvement under the flag of the United Nations – "countries friendly to Israel that have deep experience in peacekeeping operations and would be acceptable to the Palestinians."

I can't help but cast my mind back to an interview that I conducted with John Howard after the 2001 election to recall the world before the politicisation of all things. Howard was about to set the immigration program on a course for a big Australia with the first skilled wave from China. One of the observations he made in our conversation – unremarkable at the time, but which jumps off the page now – was about the civil wars in the former Yugoslavia, which had just come to a merciful end with the termination of Slobodan Milošević's government in Belgrade. Howard marvelled at the absence of conflict in Australia's Serbian and Croatian communities. While he still had his doubts about multiculturalism, it had just passed the Balkan stress test.

"I think we have been remarkably free in this country of the importation of disputes from overseas," he told me. "We, by and large, went through the disintegration of Yugoslavia without too much trouble breaking out here, when you think of how many hundreds of thousands of Serbians, Croatians and other people of Yugoslav descent are here."

One of the differences then was that it never occurred to Labor, or to the Australian Democrats, to light a flare for one or other side in that bloody conflict. Not even Pauline Hanson thought to go there. The arguments over the Voice and Gaza reflect our times. Australians today are quicker to anger, after the multiple shocks of fire, flood, plague and inflation. But the responsibility of leaders is to absorb that anger and address its underlying causes. What we have, instead, is an unthinking escalation from the right and left, and a government on mute in the middle.

It's too late now, but the window for a successful referendum on the Voice was more likely to open in the second term of an Albanese government, after Labor had seen off Dutton's politics of division. There would have been no shame in delaying the referendum once it was clear that it would fail. A strategic withdrawal would have allowed the grassroots campaign to continue without the white noise of politics. If support for the Voice recovered, and if Labor won a second term with the Liberals still shut out of the capital cities, then the case for bipartisanship would almost make itself.

The paradox for Albanese is that the defeat of the referendum undermined his own two-term strategy to consolidate power in the first and seek a mandate to become a reformist government in the second.

THE LONG SHADOWS OF HAWKE, KEATING AND HOWARD

Anthony Albanese bristles at the commentors who declare that his government is wasting its first term in office. On the razor-cold August day when I interview the prime minister in his parliamentary office, one of those critics, Sean Kelly, who served as a press secretary in the Rudd and Gillard governments, writes in the Nine Media papers about his "rule of three." Name the three most memorable events of a parliamentary term. Were they good or bad for the government? If mostly good for the government, the government won the next election. "If mostly bad, it lost."

Kelly answers his thought experiment as follows: "The referendum definitely. Inflation? Maybe … The stage-three tax cuts were a big story, but tax cuts tend to be forgotten fast." He adds climate change and an integrity commission to his list but struggles to get to three issues or events that have defined the government in the public mind. It is easier, he concludes, to remember the things that had been learnt since the last election about the previous government. The horrible findings of the "Robodebt" royal commission. The ongoing legal drama involving former Liberal staffers Bruce Lehrmann and Brittany Higgins. And the secret ministries Scott Morrison awarded himself during the pandemic, including the Treasury.

I mention the Kelly column to Albanese by way of asking him to respond to the observation that while his government has been busy, it is risk-averse and low-key.

"He's wrong," the PM says. "He romanticises a mythical land that he lived in once."

It is true that Labor prime ministers are judged by a higher standard than their Liberal counterparts, against the impossible benchmark of reform nostalgia. Even the Hawke/Keating government, which the present generation of Labor politicians and advisers view as the gold standard for fusing progressive values with electoral success, faced the accusation of timidity in its early years. Albanese was a young staffer in lion of the left Tom Uren's office in 1985, when Gough Whitlam advised Labor that it was in the business of changing the nation, not managing it. "There are many people in the Labor party who are so frightened of putting a foot wrong that they won't put a foot forward," Whitlam said in an interview to mark the tenth anniversary of the dismissal of his government.

The shadow that Whitlam cast over his immediate successors was brief in time and benign in nature. The twin shadows of Bob Hawke and Paul Keating loomed much larger over the next two Labor governments. They extended beyond the usual pissing contests over policy achievements to the very exercise of power. Whether working in tandem or flying solo, Hawke and Keating were the last Labor leaders to compel the political system to respond to their agenda. The Hawke/Keating open economic model with the safety nets of Medicare and universal superannuation, and a mass immigration program centred in our Asian neighbourhood, survived the change of government even though John Howard had previously expressed vehement opposition to Labor's social agenda.

The fact that the monarchist Howard held a referendum on the republic was testament to the power of Keating's advocacy for change. The idea did not die with Labor's landslide defeat in 1996; Howard had to kill it in his second term, with a vote that he later acknowledged might have cost him the prime ministership. "If the republican position had been carried in 1999, my position as Prime Minister would have been weakened. Although there was a free vote for Liberal parliamentarians, the reality would have been that on a fundamental constitutional issue the Liberal Prime Minister of the day would have been seen as out of step with public opinion."

Howard eventually outran the shadows of Hawke and Keating with his third election victory in 2001, in a campaign that simultaneously removed the threat of Pauline Hanson's One Nation party on his right flank and convinced Labor that it could not return to office without accepting his version of national identity.

Rudd and Gillard do not have a policy reform legacy which survived the retribution of the Abbott government, apart from the National Disability

Insurance Scheme. Far from being a mythical land, the Rudd and Gillard governments serve as a visceral reminder to Albanese and his ministers of the political multiplier of missed opportunities – six wasted years in office, punished by nine years in Opposition.

Reflecting on Labor's implosion when in power, Albanese nominates the fumbling of emissions trading in 2009–10 and the leadership rivalry between Rudd and Gillard as two of the main triggers. The points he wants to underline are that his government has a climate plan that will stick and that its ministers share a "remarkable sense of purpose and unity."

"I have no doubt that part of that discipline is because so many senior members have seen the movie," he says. "They know how it ends, because they went through it. Then they had to wait three terms to come back to sit around the cabinet table."

Labor's two longest-serving governments – the thirteen years of Hawke and Keating and the eight years of Curtin and Chifley – also shared the discipline of lived experience. The leaders and senior ministers of those governments had been members of their doomed and divided predecessors, namely the Whitlam and Scullin governments. And like Albanese's government, they had replaced discredited Coalition governments that would not pose an immediate electoral danger from Opposition.

This is where the past provides the clue to what has been missing in twenty-first-century Labor: the confidence to change the country in the first term of government. The defining moments of the Curtin and Hawke governments came within a year of taking power. Less than three months separated John Curtin's swearing-in as the prime minister of a minority government in 1941 and his declaration that Australia would look to the United States for its defence, "free from any pangs as to our traditional links or kinship with the United Kingdom." Bob Hawke's government floated the dollar nine months after its election in 1983. These decisions were forced on Australia by the necessities of war and economic crisis. Yet both leaders had also implemented their most cherished social policy goal within that first year in office. Curtin had secured full employment by placing the economy on a full wartime footing. Hawke delivered Medicare.

Neither Rudd in 2007 nor Albanese in 2022 took a program to the electorate that was comparable in political risk with Medicare, which the Coalition opposed and would continue to fight after its implementation. Instead, Labor's campaign platforms included policies written for them by their opponents. Rudd matched the tax cuts Howard announced in the first week of the campaign, even though they risked higher interest rates and would leave a structural hole in the budget. Albanese, likewise, was saddled with Scott Morrison's stage-three tax cuts.

Albanese took the copycat approach even further. Rudd had allowed himself the flexibility to soften Howard's asylum seeker policy. Albanese did not want any product differentiation at all.

"At the last election they said we'd open the borders, we wouldn't push back boats. On national security, we wouldn't support AUKUS. We'd be soft on China. We can't be trusted on the economy."

He ticks off each item of the scare campaign. "Operation Sovereign Borders is in place – no one has been settled here. On international affairs, we have repaired the relationship with China, the relationship with ASEAN, with the Pacific Island Forum, all of that is a positive. AUKUS is going ahead. On the economy, that has gone [well] too – two budget surpluses, something they never produced."

Labor people can read between the lines. He is not merely comparing his government's achievements to the caricature drawn by the Coalition. He is inviting comparison with the record number of boat arrivals and near-record budget deficits which undermined the credibility of the Rudd and Gillard governments.

Yet this leaves Albanese trapped on the sticky wicket of the Howard era, defining his own Labor government, in part, by its ability to defend the policies of its Coalition opponents.

To be fair to both Albanese and Rudd, the small-target strategy for winning government had been predetermined for them by the defeat of previous Opposition programs with too many targets – Bill Shorten's in 2019 and Mark Latham's in 2004. And those Labor victories followed the rules already established by John Howard in 1996, when he minimised the policy disagreements between himself and Paul Keating so that he could make the election a referendum on an unpopular prime minister.

Albanese is correct to claim leadership stability and orderly cabinet processes for vetting policies as advances on Rudd's first term, and he won't make Gillard's mistake of seeking a second term on a reduced Labor agenda that ruled out, for example, further action on climate change. Also, he has a better read of Dutton's negative line and length than Rudd had of Abbott's, despite being wrongfooted on the Voice.

But these in-house evaluations can only go so far, because Albanese is about to enter the uncharted Labor territory of asking permission to be a reformer in his second term. The only prime minister to pull this off was Howard, who switched from a small target in 1996 to campaigning for a goods and services tax in 1998.

*

John Howard and Anthony Albanese were the last men standing in their respective parties when they won government. Fifteen of Howard's twenty-two years in parliament before his election triumph had been served in Opposition to the governments of Whitlam, Hawke and Keating. Twenty of Albanese's twenty-six years were spent shaking his fist at the governments of Howard, Abbott, Turnbull and Morrison.

Howard realised early on that his landslide majority was brittle. The electorate was surly, and its mood swings difficult to anticipate and placate. He did have the nation's undivided attention following the Port Arthur massacre in April 1996, and rose to that awful occasion with gun law reform. But his policy-lite platform left the government with little else to do after the Senate passed Peter Costello's first budget.

Howard created a vacuum of authority for himself, which the media happily filled with populists. The independent MP Pauline Hanson emerged as a competitor to his right, and in 1997 formed her own party, One Nation. Later that year, the leader of the Australian Democrats, Cheryl Kernot, created a disruption from the left by defecting to the Labor Party. Hanson was grabbing primary votes from the Coalition and Labor. Kernot helped push Liberal voters to the Labor column.

At first, Howard did not wish to insult Hanson's supporters. He tiptoed around her race provocations against First Australians and Asian Australians by disagreeing with her on the detail while defending her right to free speech. That only encouraged Hanson to go further to the right. Howard took his time to solve the riddle. He could not compete with her, or accommodate her. He had to isolate her by picking a fight with Labor on tax reform.

Liberal pollster and strategist Mark Textor explained the thinking in an interview for my ABC documentary *Making Australia Great*: "Why did Hanson flat-foot Howard? Because Howard, after attacking Keating from the right, was being attacked from the right for the first time."

Howard needed something to sell, on his terms, not hers, to "repolarise" the electorate into a "left versus right [contest] on the economy." He reached back to the GST, which he had previously advocated for without success as treasurer to Malcolm Fraser and which had been rejected by the Australian people at the 1993 election.

> We had to refocus the agenda on an economic agenda, not Hanson's fragmented social agenda. You couldn't just do that by having a normal economic plan, you had to have what the movie-makers would call a bit of tension in there. And that was the intuition of John Howard.
>
> He said [the GST] gave his pollster a heart attack, and it certainly did for a while. But it had enough tension to take the tension off Pauline Hanson's social debate and move the tension into an economic debate, which was much safer territory for John Howard given that he was a former treasurer and knew the stuff intimately.

Albanese had a similar epiphany, though perhaps without realising it, after the defeat of the Voice. The decision to break his election promise and rework the stage-three tax cuts in line with Labor values had the temporary effect of forcing all sides to respond to the government's agenda, on the government's terms.

Howard first floated the GST as an option in May 1997, just a month after Hanson launched her protest party. The decision to take the GST to the next election – effectively asking voters to give him permission to break his earlier promise that it would "never, ever" be Coalition policy again – came after One Nation made its stunning debut at the Queensland state election of June 1998.

Queensland National Party premier Rob Borbidge understood the existential threat that Hanson posed to his minority Coalition government. The Nationals had already lost a third of its paid party membership because of Howard's gun reforms, and many were preparing to defect to One Nation. Borbidge wanted Hanson's start-up party placed last on how-to-vote cards, but the organisational wings of the Nationals and Liberals ignored his advice and condemned the government to an electoral hiding.

One Nation seized five seats from the Nationals, and six from the Labor Opposition. Tellingly, One Nation's haul of eleven seats gave it two more than the Liberals, who surrendered six seats of their own to Labor. This allowed Labor to emerge victorious with the same number of seats as it had started with: forty-four in a parliament of eighty-nine. Peter Beattie did not need to bargain with One Nation to form a minority government, as one of the two independents, Peter Wellington, obliged with the extra vote he required.

The shock Hanson administered at the state level was a harbinger of what was to come for the federal parliament from 2010 onwards – a third-party wrecking ball that took seats from both major parties.

The Queensland result forced Howard to look back to the cities for his salvation. He had been threatening a race-based election over the High Court's *Wik* native title decision. Hanson's success killed that option.

The identity trap that Howard recognised, and avoided, in 1998 was the one Morrison couldn't see in front of him in 2022: the Liberals can't form majority government with the Nationals if they move too far to the right and alienate their traditional middle-class constituency in the cities, the so-called "forgotten people" on whom Robert Menzies had based the party.

The irony is that Howard reached back to the examples of Hawke and Keating to save his government from the ignominy of losing office after a single term. By showing both sides of the budget – the sacrifice which would pay for the fistful of dollars he would offer – Howard gave voters the respect they had been accustomed to under the previous Labor government. He was appealing to a collective good, for which they would receive individual compensation. No government or Opposition since has been able to convince Australians of the virtue of paying a new tax to fund government services.

Textor said: "What we decided to do was not sell the detail of the policy but sell the fact that the policy represented true leadership which was reflecting the best part of the Keating years and the Hawke years."

Howard had the luxury of a budget surplus to sweeten his GST package with generous tax cuts for the Liberal base – middle- and high-income families with Dad in full-time work and Mum at home raising young children; small business operators; and self-funded retirees.

Kim Beazley's Labor Party needed twenty-six seats to form majority government in 1998. It fell just eight seats short, with a slightly higher primary vote than the Coalition. The third-party vote was 20.1 per cent, then the highest of the post-war era. One Nation took almost half that total – 8.4 per cent – but was left without a seat in the House of Representatives because the Coalition parties had placed Hanson last on their how-to-vote cards.

I've teased out these results to establish the second-term reform challenge for Albanese's government, and to highlight the structural shift in the electorate which makes Labor's task many degrees more difficult than it was for the Coalition in 1998. Hanson did not have the credibility to contribute to the GST debate. Labor's minor-party competitor, the Greens, are rivals in economic and environmental policy. The Greens may not wish to return to their 2009 selves, when they stood with the Abbott-led Opposition to block the Rudd government's emissions trading scheme. But they will try to outflank Labor on climate change and housing affordability, knowing that younger voters won't punish them for demanding more of the government. Albanese's second-term mandate will be contested in both chambers of parliament. Howard's GST was mediated by the Australian Democrats, who supported tax reform but with food made tax-free. They were a moderating influence who saw their role as improving government policy, not replacing it with their own agenda.

Hanson presented, and was received, as something shockingly new to our system. But her protest vote spiked and then collapsed more quickly than the previous third-party cycles for the Democratic Labor Party and the Australian Democrats. One Nation's primary vote almost halved to 4.3 per cent in 2001 and then crumbled to just 1.2 per cent in 2004. Hanson found a more crowded third-party field on her return to politics as a senator in 2016. Fellow Queenslander Clive Palmer was competing alongside her on the right for the protest votes of former Coalition and Labor supporters. Their combined share at the last election was 9.1 per cent, just above One Nation's high-water mark of 1998.

The Greens have recorded a primary vote above 10 per cent in four of the past five federal elections. This, in turn, jammed Labor's primary vote in the low thirties. It is the key shift in the operating environment for Albanese compared to Howard. The Greens are able to win seats in the people's chamber, the House of Representatives, with candidates who did not enjoy a national profile before their election, unlike Hanson and later Palmer, who built parties around their personalities.

*

The Greens represent a split with more permanence for Labor than its crippling internal argument with the Catholic right in the 1950s and '60s. The DLP did not take a single lower-house seat from Labor. But the preferences it sent to the Coalition thwarted Labor in two winnable elections – the credit squeeze campaign of 1961 and Gough Whitlam's first campaign in 1969.

The DLP veto of Labor does bear some resemblance to the barrier to majority government that the teals and Greens present for the Coalition at the moment. Twelve of the sixteen seats won by the crossbench at the last election were previously held by the Coalition.

But this observation cuts both ways. A minority Labor government that relies on a handful of teals and perhaps Bob Katter would be vulnerable to a counter-offer during the life of a hung parliament. The Murdoch press and the media company formerly known as Fairfax would surely oblige with constant polling of the teal electorates to track their discomfort at propping up a Labor regime.

Howard approached the 1998 campaign with a twenty-five-seat buffer. Albanese has just two seats to play with. The loss of three Labor seats in net terms would hang the next parliament; the loss of nine would drag the total below seventy seats, and potentially release the trapdoor to Opposition after a single term in office.

The Coalition requires a net gain of twenty seats from Labor and the crossbench to form majority government – two more seats than Kim Beazley's middle-of-the-road Opposition claimed in 1998. A minority Coalition government enters the realm of possibility once it matches Labor on the floor of the parliament. A net gain of twelve seats from Labor, assuming no change to the crossbench, would see the Coalition as the largest bloc, with sixty-eight seats to Labor's sixty-six.

One scenario being wargamed by Labor insiders involves the government dropping more seats to the crossbench than it does to the Opposition. They concede that the Greens could add another two or three inner-metropolitan seats to the four they already hold – one in Brisbane and up to two in Melbourne. And if Labor faces a revolt in the migrant suburbs, one or two seats could go to (and I offer this label with love and good humour for my fellow New Australians) brown independents in Sydney's west and Melbourne's west and northwest. But a cosmopolitan enlargement of the crossbench at

Labor's expense would not necessarily assist Dutton's cause. Imagine the Liberal leader, fresh off a Trumpian campaign for nuclear power, lower immigration and a ban on refugees from Gaza, presenting his case for minority government to half a dozen Greens, half a dozen teals and a handful of brown independents.

Albanese has the loss of the western Sydney seat of Fowler to independent Dai Le at the last election to remind him of the cost of taking a safe multicultural seat for granted. He says Labor won't be making the same mistake as Abbott, whose loss to independent Zali Steggall in 2019 signalled the coming teal wave of 2022.

"It's a seat-by-seat proposition, having the right candidate in the seats, being in touch, engaging on things that matter to people. I think Tony Abbott had moved away from the average views of Manly people."

It is an easy shot, but it also highlights Labor's dilemma in the age of fragmentation. When the Liberals abandon the middle, they lose their progressive base and the ability to form either majority or even minority government. When Labor sticks too close to the middle, it invites a progressive backlash to its left, and minority government whose survival may depend on a rival party.

The maintenance of a small working majority is Labor's best case at the moment, based on its internal polling. Yet a hung parliament could benefit Labor if Albanese has the luxury of picking between crossbench MPs on an issue-by-issue basis. The gap between Labor and the Coalition would need to be wide enough to survive any defections, scandals or untimely by-elections. Albanese would not want to enter into a formal agreement with crossbench MPs, as Julia Gillard did after the 2010 election. The Greens, with a sole member in the lower house and control of the Senate, enjoyed the best of worlds in that minority government – prioritising their own policies, while blocking Labor's. They helped persuade Gillard to introduce a price on carbon, which she had ruled out beforehand, and then sided with the Coalition to prevent Labor from implementing its agreement with Malaysia to exchange asylum seekers.

It was no consolation for Labor that Abbott eventually conceded that he was wrong to obstruct the so-called Malaysia Solution.

"I doubt it would have worked," he told the Samuel Griffith Society in 2016. "Still, letting it stand would have been an acknowledgement of the government of the day's mandate to do the best it could, by its own lights, to meet our nation's challenges. It would have been a step back from the hyper-partisanship that now poisons our public life."

Nor can Labor take solace from Howard's acknowledgement that Rudd's original mandate for action on climate change should have been respected by the parliament.

"In a classic case where the perfect became the enemy of the good, the Greens combined with the Liberal and National Parties in the Senate to defeat the Rudd plan, because for the Greens it did not go far enough," Howard wrote in his book *A Sense of Balance*, published after the 2022 election. "The nation was denied an emission trading scheme, something it had already voted for in 2007. It had also been part of the Coalition's manifesto for the poll."

Howard may be the founding father of Australia's twenty-first-century culture wars. But he is also an institutionalist who wishes his protégés had spared the nation, and the Coalition, "the paralysis that we have experienced on this issue over the past decade." Howard was the last beneficiary of the old 40–40–20 system, in which the balance-of-power party in the Senate practised self-restraint. When Senator Brian Harradine said after the 1998 election that he could not pass the GST, the Australian Democrats stepped in to save the reform, and by extension Howard's prime ministership. The deal to remove food from the GST was funded by reducing promised tax cuts for higher-income earners.

Anthony Albanese discovered the hidden power of that equation twenty-five years later when he reworked the Morrison government's stage-three tax cuts, and found, to almost everyone's surprise, that he could have his voice heard above the collective din of the Coalition and the Greens.

BREAKING THE OTHER SIDE'S PROMISES

There is art to breaking election promises. Only two Labor prime ministers managed to prosper by disowning their campaign platform: Bob Hawke and Anthony Albanese. Of the pair, only Albanese genuinely changed his mind. Here is my take on the inside story.

Hawke had every intention of trimming Labor's spending program immediately after the 1983 election. The circumstances that allowed him to get away with it were unique. The Treasury department provided the alibi on the day after the poll, when it advised his incoming government that the budget deficit had blown out under the Fraser government from $6 billion to a peacetime record of $9.6 billion. The cost of adding Labor's commitments would push that figure towards $10 billion. The cherry on top for Hawke was that former treasurer John Howard had been warned about the budget black hole but chose not to provide that information to the Australian people.

With his ministry not yet sworn in, Hawke and his nervous treasurer-elect, Paul Keating, informed the Australian people that it would be "irresponsible" to honour Labor's commitments after what Treasury had just told them. Only Medicare survived the subsequent spending cull.

Albanese did not have this luxury. The charter of budget honesty introduced in 1998 empowers the Treasury and finance departments to open the book during the election campaign. Albanese also gave himself no room to manoeuvre once in government. "My word is my bond," he declared just eight weeks after the election. No one would forget that. The thought he kept coming back to was Julia Gillard's 2010 promise that there would be "no carbon tax under the government I lead." He did not want to be called a liar.

While Gillard's was the cautionary tale, the closer analogy to Albanese's predicament was Keating's "L.A.W." tax cuts. Keating put them into legislation a year before the 1993 election, and two years before they were due to be paid. The cuts were to be funded by bracket creep, without sending the budget into deficit. Those assumptions could not be met, because unemployment remained higher than expected and inflation had fallen further than the government had dreamt.

Keating might have been applauded by the media if he had flagged the changes during the campaign. But his political credibility suffered when they were announced after the election, in a horror budget that still holds the record as the most unpopular from either side. The first half of the $8 billion in tax cuts was brought forward, funded by higher indirect taxes. The second phase was pushed back by two years and was to be paid into workers' superannuation accounts.

The tax cuts Albanese inherited from Scott Morrison's government had been crafted on the same terms as Keating's, as the return of future bracket creep. Where Keating gave himself two years to deliver, Morrison was pitching six years into the future.

The cuts were originally announced in 2018, when Morrison was treasurer in Malcolm Turnbull's government. They were to be paid over three stages between 1 July 2018 and 1 July 2024. The first stage was shamelessly Labor in content, aimed at lower- and middle-income earners. Stage two was also pitched to the middle. Stage three was reserved exclusively for the middle and the top of the scale. There was nothing at all for the 2.9 million taxpayers earning less than $45,000 a year. Morrison took the opportunity of his unexpected election victory in 2019 to boost stage three, making it the most expensive, and regressive, part of the package. Albanese went to the 2022 election promising to deliver that final instalment. "I meant it," he tells me. "When I was running in 2022, I didn't want it to be about the past. We're not going to repair everything that's been done [by the previous government]. We're looking forward."

But he did authorise his treasurer, Jim Chalmers, and finance minister, Katy Gallagher, to review the stage-three tax cuts after the campaign, as part of a line-by-line examination of the budget they had inherited.

"The other bit of context which people often miss," Chalmers tells me, "is the [newly installed British Prime Minister] Liz Truss and [Chancellor]

Kwasi Kwarteng almost created a financial crisis in the UK over their big swinging tax cuts for high-income earners. We're watching what's happening in the UK in a world where inflation is galloping."

The ABC's Laura Tingle, one of the few journalists left in the system who covered Keating's tax cuts ordeal, asked Chalmers in September 2022 if he was worried about the implications of the UK turmoil.

Chalmers, "in a burst of candour," said yes. "Completely authorised," he adds. "Katy and I were thinking about what, if anything, we would have to do to stage three."

They considered the option of cheaper tax cuts – pulling back the benefit at the top, giving some of that money to the middle and bottom, and pocketing the rest to help reduce the post-pandemic budget deficit. "[But] Anthony, and I think he was right to do this, decided in the end that there were other ways that we could address these challenges and that we would proceed [with stage three]." The first Chalmers budget released in October 2022, five months after the election, preserved the tax cuts in their fiscally reckless form.

The circumstances that would allow Albanese to change his mind began to coalesce around the time of the second budget, in May 2023. A small surplus was forecast for the current financial year, 2022–23, the first from either side of politics for fifteen years. A second surplus for 2023–24 would follow, while the deficit for 2024–25, when the tax cuts were due, was expected to be significantly lower than feared.

The tax cuts were no longer a drain on the budget and could be reworked without reducing the overall cost – a promise adjusted, not repudiated. But not just yet. The most pressing demand on the second budget was to provide cost-of-living relief to counter the inflation and interest-rate shocks that were threatening Labor's slim electoral majority. The treasurer did not wish to add fuel to the inflation fire with assistance that landed directly in people's pockets. Nor did he want to pass up the opportunity to restore the budget to surplus. His economic apprenticeship as a member of treasurer Wayne Swan's office during the global financial crisis had drilled into him the urgency of rebuilding that buffer against the next shock, and to counter Coalition claims that Labor was the party of debt and deficit.

Labor insiders were questioning the government's sense of purpose by mid-2023. The off-the-record finger-pointing distributed the blame between Chalmers, for his obsession with fiscal prudence, which he couldn't sell to the public, and Albanese, for calling a referendum he couldn't win. That nagging sense of drift added to the case to revisit the tax cuts. The penny had dropped for Albanese by year's end, and Chalmers was given permission to look at making stage three fairer, but on the proviso that the full amount be delivered.

The cost to Labor of honouring of Morrison's tax cuts was bound to catch up with Albanese, with or without the inflation shock to focus his attention. Stage three returned more than bracket creep to the top, while making it harder for future governments to provide meaningful tax cuts to lower- and middle-income earners. An elite worker on $200,000 was to receive an annual tax cut of $9075, compared to $1375 for someone on an upper-middle income of $100,000. A battler on $50,000 would get $125, and there would be nothing at all for those on $45,000 or less.

Tax nerds within the Albanese government understood the trap that had been set for them. Stage three favoured men in suits – chief executives, managing directors and middle managers – as well as high-income workers in advertising, public relations and sales. Scott Morrison's men. They penalised Labor's base, in particular women in casual work, and undermined Albanese's commitment to closing the gender pay gap and boosting the supply of quality jobs in childcare, aged care and disability support. Yet the prime minister spent the first half of his term preparing to implement the most un-Labor tax cuts in the party's 123-year history.

Stage three flattened the tax scales, from four bands to three. It looked neat on paper but locked in bracket creep for lower- and middle-income earners and reduced the incentives to work. We know this because Treasury highlighted the problem in the options it presented to Chalmers. The Treasury advice challenges the long-held view, promoted by the Liberals since

Howard's day, and accepted by Labor, that the so-called aspirational voters on six-figure salaries and with seven-figure mortgages should have first call on personal tax cuts. In fact, giving priority to their needs above those of lower- and middle-earners hurt the economy by holding back women. Let's call it what it is: punch-down, not trickle-down, economics.

As Treasury wrote, "When faced with the same percentage change to after-tax wages, women – particularly women with children – are more responsive in the amount they work compared to men. In addition, people with less formal education and those with lower wage potential are more responsive to changes in after-tax income than other individuals … *Delivering a tax cut to high-income individuals is expected to increase overall participation by less than a tax cut that delivers an increase in after-tax wages for those on lower incomes.*"

I've highlighted that last line because the point is not well understood by the major parties or the traditional media. The politicians who tested the electorate's thresholds of boredom in the 1990s with two campaigns devoted to the GST, and the commentators who urged them on, shared an unconscious bias towards rewarding men in full-time work, regardless of income. Denying him generous and ongoing tax cuts, the argument went, would kill his motivation to work and provoke him to minimise his tax.

Stage three exposed the fragility of the assumption that has misdirected our tax debates in an era of widening asset and income inequality. The case for bottom-up tax reform made itself once Treasury went to work on alternatives. The redesign offered cost-of-living relief for low- and middle-income earners without adding to inflation. The forecast of more hours in work for women helped seal Albanese's approval for the changes.

Every tax band had to be adjusted to guarantee a more equitable and productive mix. Everyone received a tax cut, and all those earning between $45,000 and $140,000 pocketed substantially more than they would have under stage three. The tax cut for elite earners on $200,000 was halved to $4529, while the tax cut for someone on $100,000 was raised by $804 to $2179, and a worker on $50,000 would now get $929 instead of $125.

One of the lessons of the Rudd government's spectacular implosion in the run-up to the 2010 election, which Chalmers absorbed as a staff member inside the tent, and Albanese as a minister on its periphery, was the political necessity of an orderly process for making decisions. The tax changes were presented to the expenditure review committee of the cabinet, then the full cabinet, then the full ministry, and finally the Labor caucus. If these checks had been in place in 2010, it is less likely that Rudd would have walked away from his emissions trading scheme. Rudd made that decision alone, without even taking the issue to his so-called gang of four ministers who had centralised power during the global financial crisis.

There was a second reason why the tax cuts were subjected to the most rigorous internal process in Labor memory. Chalmers was sending Albanese, a prime minister who did not necessarily trust his treasurer, on a mission of contrition. No leader likes to admit they were wrong, and only Queensland Labor premier Peter Beattie seemed to relish the exercise. Albanese had to fess up and go on the front foot, explaining why the new tax cuts were better. The detail had to be persuasive.

As Labor's caucus flew into Canberra for their meeting, the Opposition prepared its attacks and the business community issued a warning of economic Armageddon. The tax cuts "have not only been legislated: they have won support at two general elections," the Australian Industry Group, Australian Chamber of Commerce and Industry, Business Council of Australia and Minerals Council of Australia said in a joint statement. "It is easily forgotten that the first and second stages of the 2018 reform package were skewed towards lower- and middle-income taxpayers and that the full package is much more balanced."

Albanese tells me that he asked himself how Australians would react if the stage-three tax cuts appeared on 1 July 2024 as legislated, with "$106 billion of tax cuts given to people at the high end." He put the same question to the caucus at the special meeting convened on 24 January to approve the Chalmers plan. How would they explain to voters that "we feel your pain, but we are going to give the overwhelming weight of tax cuts to people who need it the least"? It made no policy or political sense to deliver a tax cut to Liberal voters on the top of the income ladder and leave nothing for Labor's heartland.

"People forget," Albanese tells me, "I copped this for days, that this was a career-ending decision. I was convinced it was absolutely the right thing to do."

Dutton called Albanese a liar on the day the changes were announced, 25 January, and demanded an early election. But he retreated within a fortnight, with a grudging acknowledgement that the new tax cuts had hit their mark.

"We're supporting taxpayers who were doing it tough," the Opposition leader told 7.30. "We support it on the basis, not of supporting his lie, but of supporting families who are hurting as a result of bad decisions he has made."

Labor did not expect him to fold so quickly. But they underestimated his pragmatic streak. Dutton was focused on the coming by-election for the outer Melbourne electorate of Dunkley. He agreed to the tax cuts so he could turn Dunkley, a safe Labor seat on a margin of 6.2 per cent, into a mini-referendum on Albanese's character. Labor had faced eight previous by-elections in government since 1983, and the average swing against it was 8.2 per cent. Absent the tax cuts, Labor might well have lost Dunkley. Instead, Labor secured a small primary-vote swing and limited the two-party swing against it to 3.5 per cent to retain the seat easily.

In fact, both sides increased their primary vote, Labor to 41.1 per cent and the Liberals to 39.2 per cent. The last time Dunkley gave the old duopoly more than 80 per cent of the combined primary vote was in 2010. The United Australia Party and One Nation did not run candidates, which lifted the Liberal vote. But the Greens did stand, and their primary vote fell by 4 per cent, the party's lowest haul in the seat since 2004. The Albanese/Chalmers tax cuts repolarised the people of Dunkley into a Labor versus Liberal contest.

The timing of the by-election gave the government an unanticipated advantage. If Albanese had waited until after the vote to announce the changes, the Coalition and Greens might well have used their numbers in the Senate to send the legislation to a committee for review. The delay might not have killed the tax cuts, but it would have diffused the announcement effect. Dunkley removed the option of grandstanding for Dutton and Bandt.

The question left hanging by the success of the tax cuts is whether Albanese can recreate this dynamic at a federal election with a reform program that compels the protest parties to his right and left to respond to his initiative, not their complaints. The GST provides one final lesson.

When Howard gambled on tax reform in 1998, Labor countered with a tax cuts package without the GST, while the Australian Democrats campaigned for a modified GST. Howard set the terms of the debate, and demonstrated with his re-election that difficult reform is easier to sell from government than Opposition. The reason lay, in part, in the advantage the public service provides the incumbent to formulate policy. As Robert Menzies wrote in his second memoir, *The Measure of the Years*, "The truth is that a Government is made up of ministers with a far closer knowledge of the problems of their departments and a far greater access to papers and expert advice than an Opposition can have. An attack upon them must therefore be made not on the spur of the moment, but with careful preparation after a careful choice of subject matter."

Howard gave himself a year to prepare the ground for his GST, using many of the same public servants whom Paul Keating had previously tasked to find holes in the Coalition's Fightback! manifesto. Keating had fourteen months to attack Fightback! before calling the 1993 election. Labor in Opposition had only a fortnight to respond to the detail of Howard's GST before he called an early election. While Labor's tax package was more generous at the margin, it lacked gravitas. The scare campaign against the GST sounded whiney the second time around.

The Rudd government's rush-release of its proposal to tax the excess profits of mining companies in 2010 offers a counter-example of incumbency squandered. Chalmers explained what went wrong in his 2013 book, *Glory Daze*, which reflected on his time as an adviser to treasurer Wayne Swan in the Rudd and Gillard governments. He conceded that they had left it too late to design the mining tax, consult with industry and prepare the public "for a reform of this size." "Ideally, we would have had a longer run-up and a better sense of the first iteration of the tax before we announced our intention to implement it," Chalmers wrote.

The policy crisis that Labor inherited from the Coalition which offers the greatest electoral return against policy risk is housing affordability. The measures most likely to repolarise the housing debate on Labor's terms are the removal of or reduction in tax concessions for property investors. They have provided an unfair advantage for property investors over first home buyers since Howard halved the tax on capital gains in 1999. That gift to higher-income earners fused with negative gearing to ignite a house price boom which contributed to a historic decline in home ownership. Labor has already lost two elections to the cause of capital gains and negative gearing reform, in 2016 and 2019, under Shorten's leadership. Albanese ruled out those policies at the last election and continued to do so at the time of writing. But if the past does inform the present, then he should follow Howard's GST example, and his own on the stage-three tax cuts, and go to the next election with a housing reform package that shows both sides of the budget: the savings from winding back tax breaks for property investors and the personal tax cuts they would fund for all workers.

When I lamented the end of the reform era in Quarterly Essay 40, published in the wake of the 2010 federal election, I pinpointed the 2001 campaign as the turning point to a more trivial politics.

John Howard responded to warnings of electoral doom with a panic of handouts in the first half of that year. He amended the GST by cutting the fuel excise, doubled the first home-owner grant for his battlers and aspirational voters, and showered older voters with benefits not available to anyone else. Howard buried his old economic reform self and sought a new mandate as a wartime leader following the September 11 terror attacks on the United States, while retaining his side hustle in materialist populism.

The Howard handouts pushed the budget back into deficit after the 2001 election, but the fiscal hole quickly repaired itself, as if by magic. The China-led resources boom began generating windfall surpluses, which Howard raided for his successful re-election campaign in 2004 and the one he lost in 2007. None of the bribes offered to voters in this period came with offsetting savings for the budget. They left a maze of entitlements and distorted market signals which stored up problems for the future, most notably in the housing sector, where prices boomed beyond the reach of the middle class, and in public infrastructure, which could not keep up with population growth.

Labor's unforced policy errors on climate change and the mining tax in 2010 felt like the culmination of a decade-long trend which reduced the relationship between government and citizen to the question: how can I buy your support?

What I underestimated, because I had no domestic precedent to drawn on, was the role that the 2007–08 global financial crisis played in distorting public expectations of government. It created a bubble of trust in our leaders and institutions, which burst once the existential threat passed. At the time I blamed the collapse in trust on Kevin Rudd's decision to walk away from the "great moral challenge" of climate change, which he made after reading an article by Lenore Taylor in *The Sydney Morning Herald*. But that explanation only covers the initial defection of Labor voters to the Greens in 2010. With the hindsight of the pandemic, I can see that much larger forces were at play which would have rattled even the most competent government: the same forces which threaten to hang the parliament again.

The GFC triggered a new super-cycle in our politics – pro-incumbent in the crisis and anti-incumbent in the recovery – which repeated on an epic scale a decade later in the mood swing from Covid-19 lockdown to reopening.

Consider first the parallels of largesse in response to the two global shocks. The Rudd government's stimulus program in 2008 involved one-off payments which exceeded any of the Howard bribes between 2001 and 2007. The public understood the transaction could not be repeated, but nonetheless resented the sacrifices that came with recovery – the budget repair and higher interest rates. The Morrison government's JobKeeper scheme and the doubling of unemployment benefits were more generous, and paid across a longer timeline, than any previous social support in our history. No subsequent tax cut or handout could hope to provide a comparable level of assistance to households, or a comparable bump in a prime minister's approval rating.

Now recall how politics was suspended during each emergency. The podium belonged to Rudd during the GFC, with no rival press conference scheduled to counter his rolling addresses to the nation. The then Opposition leader, Malcolm Turnbull, supported the first stimulus package. The head of the Treasury, who would not normally be in the public eye, briefly became a national hero; the prime minister would repeatedly cite Ken Henry's mantra to "go early, go hard, go households" to reassure voters that the billions being spent to prop up the economy had been sanctioned by rational advice.

The pandemic broadened the stage to include state and territory leaders, as the Federation intended in a health crisis. Chief health officers stepped forward in place of the secretary of Treasury and the governor of the Reserve Bank as the learned servants of the public, operating above politics.

The pandemic lifted all incumbents, regardless of their age or political colour. Five state and territory governments stood for re-election during the lockdown years of 2020 and 2021, and all five were comfortably returned. That list included the blowout in Western Australia, where Mark McGowan's Labor government won a record fifty-three of fifty-nine seats in the state parliament, including all but one in Perth. Across the Tasman, Jacinda Ardern's Labor government was returned with a majority in its own right, the first since New Zealand introduced its mixed member proportional electoral system in 1993. Ardern Labor's primary vote of 50 per cent was the highest for any party since 1951.

After the GFC of 2008–09, the hung parliament of August 2010 marked the U-turn to a much longer anti-incumbent cycle. The government of the day, whether Labor or Coalition, lost eight of the next twelve federal, state and territory elections. It is important to note that this phase of recrimination preceded Brexit and the election of Donald Trump in 2016. Australia suffered a grumpy letdown from the GFC, not the nativist revolt that was fomenting in Britain and the United States. Our version of muscular conservatism, Tony Abbott, had already been sacked by the Liberals a year before Trump secured the Republican Party's nomination for president.

The Scanlon Foundation's survey of trust in the federal government highlights the whiplash in attitudes from crisis to recovery. The share of voters who trusted the government "to do the right thing by Australians" jumped from 39 per cent in 2007 to 48 per cent in 2009, then crashed to 31 per cent in 2010.

The Australian Election Studies taken either side of the GFC found satisfaction with democracy slumped by fourteen percentage points, from 86 per cent to 72 per cent, between 2007 and 2010 under the Rudd/Gillard government, and by a further twelve points, from 72 per cent to 60 per cent, between 2013 and 2016, from Gillard back to Rudd, and from Abbott to Turnbull. The figure had settled at 59 per cent in 2019, when Morrison celebrated his miracle election win with a shout-out to the contrary state that saved his government: "How good is Queensland?" Only 25 per cent of voters surveyed after the 2019 campaign said "people in government can be trusted" – a record low for this survey.

The weird trajectory of Morrison's prime ministership tracked the pandemic's boom and bust in trust. He moved from a figure of global ridicule for taking a holiday to Hawaii during the bushfires to the statesman who kept the virus in check and delivered JobKeeper, before reverting to his polarising self, picking needless fights with Labor premiers and shifting blame for the failure of his vaccine rollout.

The Scanlon survey showed an even sharper rise in trust during Covid when compared to the GFC. Trust in the federal government soared from 36 per cent in 2019 to 56 per cent in 2020, then dropped by twelve points to 44 per cent in the second year of lockdown, and to 41 per cent after the economy reopened in 2022. Worryingly for Albanese, the decline was not halted by a change in government. Trust fell by a further five points on his watch and was back to its pre-pandemic level of 36 per cent by 2023. Voters did not resolve their post-Covid trauma when they deleted Morrison from their screens.

As we saw following the GFC, the landing from the pandemic was harder for incumbents than it was for the real economy. Government has changed hands in five of the eight elections held since reopening, even though the economy has been operating at near-full employment.

The global shocks of the twenty-first century so far have a wartime quality to them. Voters rally around their leaders, willing them on to victory, then mark the peace by changing governments. Let's call it the Churchill effect.

Inflation, on Jim Chalmers' reading, is the third great economic shock in fifteen years.

> The first one is a financial shock that becomes a demand shock. The second one is a health shock that becomes a supply shock but still has the elements of the same response as the GFC – big fiscal outlays. By the time we get to the third crisis, the antidote is very different … The answer to the first was more demand, and the answer to the third one is to try to help people, to being part of the solution without becoming part of the problem when it comes to inflation.

Inflation is an old-school economic shock, with a long history of killing governments. It damages the incumbent from the outset; there is no boom in trust which a leader can harness.

The policy levers that are pulled in a financial or health crisis – government stimulus and rapid-fire cuts in interest rates – are forced in the opposite direction to deal with inflation. The Reserve Bank squeezes consumer spending and investment with higher interest rates – raising the cost of credit to slow the increase in the cost of living. Absurd when put that way. But this is what authorities allude to when they refer to monetary policy as a blunt instrument. It lacks precision and can bludgeon an economy into recession, as the governments of Menzies, Whitlam, Fraser and Hawke could all attest. The Albanese government stands more in Whitlam's shoes than Hawke's, being without the experience of managing a previous inflation shock.

The return of inflation after a hiatus of more than thirty years has come with the added complication of a housing crisis which pre-dated the shock. As such, this bout of inflation is interpreted by voters as confirmation of an existing economic illness, not another contagion that the government can blame on the rest of the world and address with handouts. Higher interest rates make housing even more unaffordable, a case of the cure feeding the disease.

When I outline my theory of the boom and bust in trust to the treasurer, he says governments have "desensitised people to big outlays." He runs through the shopping list of support the government has delivered in its fight against inflation: "tax cuts, energy bill relief, rent assistance, JobSeeker, early childhood education, medicines. Absent those two other shocks, that would be seen as a pretty big intervention."

He mentions a question the journalist Michelle Grattan asked him – Are you disappointed you didn't get a big bump from those measures? – and shares his reply: "I don't think people are in the mood to give governments credit. Our primary motivation is getting it right."

If you follow the logic through to the next election, it means Labor does not expect votes for being prudent. More bits-and-pieces measures won't work either. And the electorate can't be bribed, Howard-style, without risking the Reserve Bank's sanction of even higher interest rates.

Although the outbreak of inflation pre-dated the federal election, the cost of fighting it has been borne by Albanese's government. Twelve of the thirteen interest-rates increases between May 2022 and November 2023 occurred under Labor. It was ever thus for Australia's oldest political party. The past six incoming Labor governments, going back to Andrew Fisher's in 1914, were confronted with a global crisis on entry to office. Only two of the six, Curtin/Chifley (1941 to 1949) and Hawke/Keating (1983 to 1996), survived long enough to claim the spoils of peace and recovery.

The Australian economy carries a second vulnerability into this inflation shock to go with our self-made housing crisis. China, our safety net during the global financial crisis, has emerged from the pandemic with the opposite challenge to the West: deflation.

What can't be known for some years is whether China's present difficulties represent a small speed bump on its historic journey to replacing the United States as the world's largest economy, or an era-defining and irreparable breakdown of its growth model. Australia's economic future depends on China's continued ascension.

The two pieces of data I watch for every year are China's share of the global economy and China's share of global population. The moment when China's share of production catches up with its population represents the first great transition, from developing economy to developed. That occurred in 2021, when the world's second-largest economy was still in lockdown. But China has taken two steps back since reopening. Its population fell in absolute terms in 2022, and India replaced it as the world's most populous nation. China's share of the global economy shrank accordingly. A second year of population loss in 2023 was accompanied by a second year of relative economic decline.

China's loss has been America's gain. The United States has increased its share of the global economy over the past two years by the equivalent amount, thus delaying, if not denying, China's dream of becoming number one. The post-Covid story, in geopolitical terms, has been the tension between the Biden boom and the Xi stagnation. The sting for China is that its numbers are beginning to look like Japan's, when the last challenge to American primacy faded.

China has scale on its side and won't suffer Japan's precipitous fall in the 1990s. It was still responsible for almost a quarter of the global economy's modest growth this year, and will continue to top up Australia's national income. Nevertheless, Australian authorities should start planning for the end of the free ride, because China now has two things in common with the Japan of the '90s. The first is China's credit bubble, which will act as a handbrake on growth for some years to come even if it doesn't burst. The second is that the Chinese labour force has reached the tipping point of ageing, when more workers leave through retirement or death than are replaced by new recruits. The Chinese labour force stopped growing in 2015.

Chalmers recalls advice Ken Henry gave during the GFC. "He presented a graph to us that basically said it's worse for us if China comes off a little bit than if the US comes off a lot – for some reason that has always hung around my mind. And we're seeing that now in the China side of the story, where commodity prices are very substantially lower than they were at the start of the year."

The first two Chalmers budgets straddled the Biden boom and Xi stagnation to return surpluses with the help of bracket creep, stronger-than-expected employment and the windfall from higher commodity prices. A third Chalmers surplus would maximise Labor's options for a re-election campaign based around a reform package with winners and losers, to ensure no one is worse off in the short term. But a third surplus appeared unlikely at the time of writing, because Australia's economy had slowed to a crawl and China's had yet to deliver its usual bonus.

The political consolation for Labor of a weaker economy is the prospect of lower interest rates. The US Federal Reserve signalled the end of its inflation fight in September with a larger-than-anticipated cut in interest rates. A more accommodating RBA won't, of itself, save the Albanese government from slipping into minority, or worse. Election-year cuts in interest rates did not spare Gillard's leadership in 2013, nor prevent Labor's landslide defeat under Rudd. But an easing in monetary policy would clear the air for a housing reform package. The question for Albanese and Chalmers is whether they are brave enough to use housing as the platform to rebuild trust in their government, and by extension the political system.

Housing is the defining failure of Australian capitalism and politics in the twenty-first century. No other part of the economy has its distortions perpetuated by bipartisan policy. Where the climate wars have veered between government support for and denial of renewable energy, government intervention in the housing market has been a constant and counterproductive feature of our national life. The construction industry, the nation's largest employer of men, is unable to build enough houses, apartments and townhouses to meet demand. The political system, across all three tiers of government, has been its accomplice in driving prices beyond the reach of the middle class, with handouts to prop up demand and restrictions on supply. A twin failure of capitalism *and* government intervention.

The old major-party duopoly clings to the assumption that elections are still decided in the mortgage belt; by the voters already in the market, not those locked out of it. That may be true for the coming campaign. But the idea that home ownership forms the undisputed centre of our politics no longer holds. The centre is increasingly occupied by young, educated Australians who may never own their own home.

Renters helped evict the Liberals from the cities in 2022, and now threaten Labor's majority at the next election. They form one part of the progressive riddle for the major parties.

Millennials born between 1981 and 1995 and Gen-Zs born after 1996 are the first groups to enter their thirties with a home ownership rate below 50 per cent. The baby boomers at the equivalent stage in their lives four decades ago had a home ownership rate of 68 per cent.

Millennials and Gen-Z are less likely to vote for the Coalition as they grow older, according to a report by political scientist Dr Shaun Ratcliff.

"However, the main beneficiary of this since the 2000s appears to be The Greens, not Labor," he wrote. "The political divergence between the generations has been driven by real social and material differences. Millennials are more likely to have a university education than older cohorts, and fewer are hitting the milestones in their 20s and 30s that may have been associated with increasing support for conservative parties as voters age, such as home ownership and family formation."

The other group challenging the major parties from the centre are the teals. As well as renters, their voters happen to include property investors who abandoned the Liberals over climate change and treatment of women. The duopoly was not designed for an electorate in which the mortgage belt faces rivals for political influence from both ends of the property ladder – the renter and the landlord.

A clear line can be drawn from the Howard-era concessions for property investors in the late 1990s to the progressive revolt at the last election. It can be measured, socially and politically, in the drop in the national home ownership rate and the corresponding rise of the landlord class.

The housing market now breaks into unequal thirds. Renters are 31 per cent of households, on almost equal electoral footing with those who own their home outright on 32 per cent. The last census put both camps at around 2.9 million households. The mortgage belt is still the largest bloc, comprising 3.3 million, or 35 per cent of all households.

The landlord class has seen its ranks grow by almost one million, from 1.286 million, or 12.3 per cent of taxpayers in 1998–89 – the year before Howard introduced the discount for capital gains – to 2.268 million, or 14.6 per cent of taxpayers in 2021–22.

The catch-22 for Albanese's government is that removing the Howard-era tax distortions cannot return us to the late 1990s, when the national home ownership rate was still at its post-war high of 71 per cent. Tax reform, however it is designed, would have only a marginal effect on prices, and does not address the supply constraints at the heart of the housing crisis. But it would send a political signal to younger Australians that the government is on its side. Labor seemed to be heading in this direction when the Nine newspapers reported in September that Treasury had been tasked to review the capital gains tax concession and negative gearing. It was read as a kite-flying exercise by the press gallery after the prime minister confirmed the substance of the report. "I'm sure the public service are looking at policy ideas. That's because we value them."

The leak wasn't authorised, but nor was it malicious, from what I can gather. Nevertheless, it had the unintended consequence of killing all options for reform. The leak came too soon for the government to know where it wanted to take the debate, and too close to the next election to leave the issue hanging and invite a pincer of scare campaigns from the Coalition on behalf of investors, and the Greens on behalf of renters.

Albanese's prospects for re-election may not have died at this point, but the clumsy exercise in raising, then dashing, hopes for reform will have reduced Labor's chances in the contest with the Greens for younger voters, and increased the Coalition's confidence that it can drag Labor back to its level, as one of the big minority parties in a hung parliament.

The prime minister threw beach sand in the gears of the campaign in October with his private decision, not flagged to colleagues, to buy a $4.3-million home on a clifftop with uninterrupted views of the Pacific Ocean. The purchase of the mansion on the hill with his fiancée, Jodie Haydon, was, many critics agreed, tone-deaf. Some compared it to Scott Morrison's Hawaiian adventure during the Black Summer of fire. That may be a stretch, but it did draw attention to the great housing divide between the parliament and the people. One in three members and senators, across all parties, own at least three properties, compared to around 4 per cent of taxpayers.

The accidental narrowing of Labor's re-election platform provided an insight into a curious feature of the forty-seventh parliament. The housing crisis, as all sides call it, has united Labor, the Coalition and the Greens in performative gridlock. Labor has been inviting the Greens to obstruct whenever it presented housing legislation to the Senate, and the Coalition would ensure a standoff by siding with the Greens in an unholy alliance of opposites. The fourth side in the parliament, the teals, were cut out of this argument because their numbers were confined to the House of Representatives, where the Albanese government had no need of them.

Of the three combatants, Labor had taken a modest but considered election platform to the people in 2022 which promoted public housing and private ownership for low- and middle-income earners. The Greens' program – to build one million public and community homes paid for by a tax on billionaires – was more slogan than serious policy, because no major party would implement it on their behalf in a hung parliament. The Coalition was too slow to appreciate the importance of the issue and left it until the last week of the 2022 campaign to announce their policy, a rehash of an old idea to let first home-buyers raid their superannuation savings to help fund a deposit. As the Loughnane/Hume review noted, "The sense the [Morrison] Government had 'run its race' was allowed to develop as a result."

When Labor introduced its $10-billion public housing fund to the Senate in 2023, the Greens threatened to block it with the help of the Coalition. Labor called their bluff. It was the fight government insiders tell me they had been itching to have with the Greens, to demonstrate the unreasonableness of their rival on the left. A compromise was eventually reached after a delay of three months. The next piece of Labor's program, the Help to Buy shared equity scheme, was also presented to be defeated. Labor wanted to put the scheme to a vote, to record the opposition of the Greens. The Greens and the Coalition deferred that vote, and at the time of writing the legislation remained stalled in the Senate.

The contrived nature of these disputes over the smaller parts of Labor's electoral mandate belies what has, in fact, been a relatively productive parliament. The Greens took the pragmatic decision immediately after the last election to pass every plank of the government's climate change program. Labor and the Coalition, meanwhile, were able to find common ground in 2024 to reform the National Disability Insurance Scheme and aged care. Albanese's government has not faced the level of obstruction endured by Rudd and Gillard on climate change and asylum seeker policies, or Whitlam on Medibank, the forerunner of Medicare.

But Labor is being bombarded with blame for a crisis it inherited from the Coalition. Dutton wants to drag the discussion back to migration.

"It's not just housing," he told ABC TV's *7.30* in May 2024. "People know that if you move suburbs, it's hard to get your kids into school, or into childcare. It's hard to get into a GP because the doctors have closed their books. It's hard to get elective surgery. These factors have all contributed to capacity constraints because of the lack of planning in the migration program."

There were two technical problems with this argument. First, house prices surged during lockdown. Second, the decision to reopen the international border without constraints was made by the unloved and unmourned Morrison government. The Coalition removed the cap on working hours for international students in January 2022 to help fill labour shortages in the economy. Labor has since reimposed the cap and, more controversially, proposed to limit the number of new international students universities can enrol in 2025.

Both sides are taking a risk with the same New Australian community. Young Indian families typically settle in the outer suburbs. They are not responsible for the affordability crisis; on the contrary, their demand is adding to the housing stock, especially in Melbourne's west and north-west. Indian students land as renters, not buyers, and they gravitate to the university suburbs of the inner city, where they are more willing than the local-born to live in shared accommodation. The finger of suspicion pointed by Dutton, and to a lesser extent by Albanese, is not just unfair on the Indian community. It undermines their faith in the political system, pushing a Labor-leaning voter into none-of-the-above.

New house prices, as measured in the Consumer Price Index, surged by 20 per cent in 2021–22, before Labor took office. They rose by an additional 7.8 per cent – just above the inflation rate of 6 per cent – in the first twelve months of Albanese's government, before levelling off. The punchline is that prices actually fell slightly in real terms in 2023–24 across our three most populous cities – in Sydney and Melbourne, the twin capitals of New Australia, and in Brisbane, the main destination for internal migration. A boom with the border closed, which eases once the migrants come flooding in. No one would have had that run of numbers on their bingo card for the Australian economy before the pandemic.

The Morrison housing boom was an unexpected side effect of lockdown itself and the working-from-home revolution. The Grattan Institute's Brendan Coates described the trend as a "race for space."

"People want more space to themselves, either by taking an extra bedroom as a home office or by moving out of the family home or a share house," he wrote in 2023. "The Reserve Bank estimates that the number of Australians living in each home fell from an average of 2.55 people in late 2020 to 2.48 people by mid-2022. That change alone implies we need an extra 275,000 homes just to house the existing population."

The construction industry met this additional demand with fewer houses. Just 173,000 new dwellings were completed in 2023 – the lowest number in a decade.

"Construction is taking longer to complete," according to the State of the Housing System report delivered to the Albanese government in 2024. "The average time from approval to completion for a new house is around 12 months, up from 9 months in 2019–20. New townhouses currently take around 15 months from approval to completion and new apartments around 29 months."

The twin failures of the housing market and government intervention belonged to the Coalition, but the consequences were Labor's to manage. What surprised me when I crunched the data was the resilience of the broader economy. Albanese's government has presided over the fastest rate of job creation for any new government, Labor or Coalition, on record. Total employment grew by 835,000, or 6.2 per cent, between May 2022 and May 2024, beating the previous record of 5.5 per cent for Bob Hawke's government. The rate of growth was double that of the incoming governments of Howard, Rudd and Abbott.

The new jobs have been split 50/50 between men and women, with construction and energy driving the bloke economy, and health care and social assistance dominating the female side.

Imagine what Paul Keating or Peter Costello would have made of these numbers.

*

The impasse on housing highlights the inherent instability of a hung parliament in dealing with long-term challenges. The housing crisis is too big to fix within a single term, which makes it almost too easy to politicise for short-term gain. But that politicisation risks alienating the very voters who broke the duopoly at the last election, and with it the constituency for a new era of reform.

Labor has boxed itself into the corner of incrementalism, with a prime minister from its Left who carries himself more like Howard than Whitlam, Hawke or Keating. The contradiction is partly born of Albanese's political rise through the back rooms of deal-making, not the front stage of debate and persuasion. The dominant side of Albanese's political identity is that of factional warrior. Like Howard's, that identity was forged within a minority tribe. The NSW Right had lorded it over Albanese's Left faction in the 1980s and '90s. Howard's apprenticeship was served as a NSW conservative when the Victorian moderates ran the country under Menzies and then Fraser. Each in his way came into office without needing to inspire the electorate, because the Australian people were sick of the incumbent. In Albanese's case that creates a particular dilemma when the voters who broke the duopoly want to be inspired.

His politics may be progressive, but his approach is defensive. He speaks in dot points in our interview when describing the framework for his re-election program – "the four themes that everything fits into."

"Cost of living, is it making a difference there? Strengthening Medicare. A future made in Australia. And our place in the world."

He elaborates: "What does future growth look like? What do optimism and hope look like? Seizing the opportunities of the changes in the global economy. That's making more things here, that's advanced manufacturing jobs, that's regional growth, that's transforming our existing fossil-powered economy into a renewable energy superpower. A lot of it is about manufacturing and traditional trades, but new industries as well."

The substance is Labor, but the language is managerial, more premier than prime minister. He lacks the poetry of his predecessors. A competent machine man in the Lodge is no bad thing after the chaos and inactivity of the Abbott, Turnbull and Morrison governments. But the nation faces a multiplicity of challenges. The domestic list alone requires a decade-long incumbency to address, from the great shortages of housing and infrastructure to the supply of labour for the care economy; from the energy transition to food security.

Albanese has yet to find his leader's voice. The clarity of purpose that came with the reworking of the stage-three tax cuts proved to be temporary. He remains a progressive prime minister in waiting, caught between the hybrid Labor/Coalition program he took to the last election and the reform program he is still finalising for a second term. Trust in his government has to be restored the hard way, in an anti-incumbent cycle.

The danger of a hung parliament for Albanese is that the crossbench would claim a mandate to replace Labor's program with its own. The performative gridlock of the first term could become a permanent feature of the second.

The former trade union leader Bill Kelty, long regarded as the third-most powerful member of the Hawke/Keating government, has suggested a way forward on housing: the creation of a new National Housing Commission that builds houses in conjunction with the states.

> For many young people it is the likelihood that they will be forever renters in a market of forever shortages that destroys ambition. Abandon any idea of subsidies; they don't work except to increase prices. What we need is a modified Singapore model in which government, banks and superannuation provide the capital to build generational houses for public and social needs. The nation has to stop the baloney and replace false promises with real buildings.

Albanese would say he is already doing just that, with his $32-billion "Homes for Australia" plan. But that brings us back to the question of the leader's voice. The PM gets no credit for what he is already doing because voters do not see the big picture he thinks he is painting for them. The problem, as Kelty points out, is one of ambition. The sales pitch is timid because the ideas are stale. "The Labor Party is a long way from done but at the moment it is mired in mediocrity that is not much different from the past generation."

There is an equivalent staleness to Peter Dutton's attack on Labor. It is more Home Affairs and Defence than kitchen-table economics. Dutton often refers to the "forgotten Australians" in his speeches, in a nod to "the creator of our great party, Robert Menzies," but he rarely mentions housing policy. It's a curious omission because Menzies defined the importance of the forgotten people to Australia's stability through their principal asset, the family home. The middle class, he said, "has 'a stake in the country'. It has responsibility for homes – homes material, homes human, homes spiritual."

Remember that Menzies delivered his radio sermons in Opposition, at a time of war when only Victoria and South Australia had a majority of their people living in capital cities. Farmers formed a larger part of the middle class that Menzies had in mind than the "professional men and women" he represented in the seat of Kooyong. Today, women with tertiary degrees – the teals' middle class – are the nation's largest group of workers. Dutton ignores them at his and the Liberal Party's peril.

Demography is not on Dutton's side. Sydney holds two-thirds of the population of New South Wales, and Melbourne, Perth and Adelaide are approaching 80 per cent of their respective state populations. Only Queensland and Tasmania have a majority of their people still living outside the capital. The Liberals cannot afford to treat the teal electorates as an anomaly of inner-city wokeness that can be ignored in pursuit of a new mythical middle in the outer suburbs. The political centre has been moving towards the CBD, not away from it, and to voters who are being denied the Menzies dream of home ownership.

Success at the next election for crossbench MPs can be measured two ways. First, claiming and then holding a seat from a major party. Second, using that local voice to influence national policy.

The Greens have never let a government mandate get in the way of their own platform. It will pain Albanese and his ministers to concede this, but the incentive for the Greens to disrupt a minority Labor government will be far greater than it was in 2010. As an electoral competitor to Labor, the Greens have an interest in picking as many fights as possible.

Jim Chalmers acknowledges this point. "[The Greens'] messaging priority is people who can't find an affordable rental. Their political priority is to stop us building affordable rentals and being successful in the constituencies where the clash is [Labor] red on green."

This realisation has already seen Labor bypass the parliament and address housing supply more directly with the states through the national cabinet process. Chalmers draws a contrast between the challenges of a fractured electorate and society, and the Hawke/Keating reform era, when agreements could be reached outside the parliament between business and unions which would be respected by the Senate. "I resist the comparison sometimes because I don't want to say it was easier or harder, or make assessments of Paul [Keating]'s wonderful Treasurership, but if Anthony or I could get three or five people into a room and bash out a whole lot of agreements that would stick in the Senate, we'd do that."

The teals, whose constituency is closer to the traditional Australian Democrats base of small-l Liberals, loom as the more pragmatic force in a hung parliament. But they would be mindful of the experience of Tony Windsor and Rob Oakeshott, the two rural independents who backed Gillard in 2010. Neither stood for re-election in 2013, because they knew they would lose.

The bar of expectation has been lowered for the major parties. Minority government would represent a form of success for Labor if the crossbench is large enough to deny the Greens the outright balance of power in the lower house. A narrow majority, while not out of the question, would say more about the departure of the Liberals from the centre than Labor's hold on it.

Either way, Labor would find governing harder in a second term because of the incentives for the crossbench to mutate after the election as individuals fall out with their parties. Five senators have already quit to become independents in the forty-seventh parliament – two from the Coalition, and one each from Labor, the Greens and the Jacqui Lambie Network.

Success for the Liberals will turn on their ability to regain seats in the cities. The Liberal Party of Robert Menzies can't form majority, or minority, government if it remains outnumbered by the Queensland LNP and the Nationals within the Coalition.

My opinion, for what's it's worth, is that a hung parliament offers perhaps our last best chance to restore purpose to our politics – and policymaking. But that will depend on whether the members and senators elected to the forty-eighth parliament respect the will of the Australian people to keep our politics anchored in a problem-solving centre.

SOURCES

5 referendums … notoriously difficult to pass: Murray Goot, "Without 'bipartianship' have referendums to change the Australian constitution ever succeeded? An unnoticed success, several near-misses, and the struggle to explain why referendums fail", *Australian Journal of Politics and History*, 25 June 2024.

5 "it was the large decline": Nicholas Biddle, Matthew Gray, Ian McAllister and Matt Qvortrup, "Detailed analysis of the 2023 Voice to Parliament referendum and related social and political attitudes", ANU Center for Social and Political Attitudes, 28 November 2023, https://csrm.cass.anu.edu.au/sites/default/files/docs/2023/11/Detailed_analysis_of_the_2023_Voice_to_Parliament_Referendum_and_related_social_and_political_attitudes.pdf.

7 between 85 and 90 per cent of residents born overseas: The data is from customised tables from the 2021 census provided to me by the Australian Bureau of Statistics.

8 fallout from the 2022 election: The capital-city Liberals serving electorates outside Brisbane were reduced from twenty-six to eleven seats, while their regional counterparts had their numbers cut by two to sixteen, for a total of twenty-seven. The merged Liberal National Party in Queensland shed a further two seats in Brisbane, but retained its eighteen regional seats, leaving it with twenty-one. Add the ten National MPs to Dutton's LNP contingent, and the Liberals were the junior partner in the Coalition for the first time in their history. The party of Robert Menzies previously held forty-four of the seventy-seven seats in Scott Morrison's government. My calculations, using the Australian Electoral Commission's results maps: https://aec.gov.au/Electorates/maps.htm.

9 "not about": Andrew Bragg, quoted in James Massola and Angus Thompson, "Liberal senator calls for conscience vote on Voice after National MPs quits over No campaign", *The Sydney Morning Herald*, 23 December 2022.

10 Australia's post-war development is mirrored in these changes: The redistribution of electoral boundaries followed the population northwards, adding six seats to Queensland's total between 1987 and 2010, and subtracting three from New South Wales and another two from Victoria. The shuffle of seats contributed to the gridlock of the past decade. The Coalition's super-majorities in Queensland sent Julia Gillard's government into minority in 2010, and ensured narrow majorities for the governments of Malcolm Turnbull in 2016 and Scott Morrison in 2019, even though Labor won a majority of seats in both Victoria and New South Wales in all three campaigns.

11 Their numbers increased by almost 1.2 million: Based on exclusive data supplied to me by the Australian Bureau of Statistics.

11 Melbourne and Sydney represent the fourth phase: Time will tell if either Victoria or New South Wales reclaim their former status, or if, on the other hand, the electorate has become so fractured than no new centre emerges. But the past does tell us what distinguished the progressive era from the conservative eras of Menzies and Howard. Menzies did not win a majority in Sydney in any of the seven successful elections he contested between 1949 and 1963. Howard did not have a majority in either Sydney and Melbourne in his four election victories between 1996 and 2004. But every government in between, from Harold Holt's in 1967 to Paul Keating's in 1993, carried both Sydney and Melbourne.

12 "The swing against the Liberal Party": Brian Loughnane and Jane Hume, *Review of the 2022 Federal Election*, Liberal Party of Australia, December 2022, https://cdn.liberal.org.au/2022/2022_election_review.pdf.

12 Only Aboriginal and Torres Strait Islanders recorded a higher level of support: Eighty-three per cent were either a hard or soft "Yes," according to the polling from YouGov.

13 "It would seem": Biddle, Gray, McAllister and Qvortrup, "Detailed analysis".

13 Only three capitals and two regional cities returned a "Yes" result: Based on the Australian Electoral Commission data.

13 Sydney's transformation from "Yes" to "No": My calculations, based on the Australia Electoral Commission's data for the two referendums: "National results", Australian Electoral Commission, 2 November 2033, https://results.aec.gov.au/29581/Website/ReferendumNationalResults-29581.htm; "1999 referendum report and statistics", AEC, https://aec.gov.au/Elections/referendums/1999_Referendum_Reports_Statistics/summary_republic.htm.

16 By opposing the Voice, Dutton gifted the teals and Greens: All seven teal and all four Green electorates voted "Yes," as did Clark, based around Hobart, which is held by independent Andrew Wilkie. The only exception on the urban cross-bench was Fowler, in Sydney's west, which the independent Dai Le won from Labor at the last election. Fowler had been the only western Sydney seat to vote for the republic in 1999.

17 "The Liberal Party is": Loughnane and Hume, *Review of the 2022 Federal Election*.

17 "Younger Australians": Biddle, Gray, McAllister and Qvortrup, "Detailed analysis".

17 whether the rejection of the Voice in the migrant suburbs cancels the progressive realignment of 2022: The Loughnane/Hume review divided the electoral map into four zones to highlight the importance of the capitals. The defeat of the Morrison government left the Liberals with just four out of forty-five inner-metropolitan seats, and sixteen of the forty-two outer-metropolitan seats (fifteen after the loss of Aston). The Coalition were also in the minority outside the capitals, with ten of the twenty-four provincial seats (nine after Andrew Gee quit the Nationals). "The only demographic class where the Liberal Party and National Party have a strong hold is in rural electorates," the report stated.

19 Menzies, Whitlam and Hawke: Menzies lost the 1951 referendum on communism, held early in his second term. Whitlam lost the prices and incomes referendum in 1973, and all four electoral reform referendum questions he put to the people in conjunction with the 1974 federal election, which Labor won. Hawke lost the electoral reform referendum held in conjunction with the 1984 election, and the four questions he put in the 1988 referendum.

19 "cared a good deal": Biddle, Gray, McAllister and Qvortrup, "Detailed analysis".

20 "Consistent feedback": Peter Lewis, "Australians have lost so much faith in government that just being heard feels like special treatment", *Guardian Australia*, 13 August 2024.

22 "The statement was issued": Phillip Coorey, "'Words matter': ASIO warns social cohesion at risk", *Australian Financial Review*, 12 October 2023.

22 "I get robust political debate": Julia Abbondanza, "'Be careful': Australia's spy chief urges politicians to avoid 'inflamed language'", SBS News, 11 August 2024.

23 "to those who keep distorting my words": Peter Dutton in Niki Savva, "Peter Dutton's immigration debate keeps heat off NSW Liberal Party", *The Sydney Morning Herald*, 5 September 2024.

23–4 "unconditionally condemned": Naveen Razik, "'Race-baiting McCarthyism": Eric Abetz slammed for asking Chinese Australians to denounce Communist Party during diaspora inquiry", SBS News, 15 October 2020.

24 "countries friendly to Israel": Martin Indyk, "The strange resurrection of the two-state solution", *Foreign Affairs*, March/April 2024.

27 "There are many people": Gough Whitlam interviewed on the tenth anniversary of the Dismissal, 11 November 1985, https://whitlamdismissal.com/1985/11/11/gough-whitlam-10th-anniversary-interview-sbs.html.

27 "If the republican position had been carried": John Howard, *Lazurus Rising*, HarperCollins, 2011, p. 377.

33 One Nation took almost half: Pauline Hanson had moved from the electorate of Oxley, which she won as independent in 1996, to contest the new seat of Blair, west of Brisbane. She recorded the highest primary vote of all the candidates – 36 per cent. But it was not enough to get her over the line. The Liberal candidate, Cameron Thompson, overtook her on preferences from the Labor and National parties.

35 The loss of three Labor seats: Labor's cause wasn't helped by the redistribution of electoral boundaries for the next election. The Melbourne seat of Higgins, which Labor won from the Liberals in 2022, was abolished, as was the teal seat of North Sydney. (As it happens, North Sydney was the only seat to return an independent candidate at the GST election in 1998.) Albanese did get some compensation with the drawing of the boundaries for the new seat of Bullwinkle in Perth, which is notionally counted as Labor's based on the booth-by-booth votes at the last election. The battle lines for the next campaign are seventy-eight Labor seats, fifty-six Coalition and sixteen on the crossbench (including six teal and four Greens MPs) in a parliament of 150. I am counting Calare as independent, but not Monash in Victoria, whose sitting member Russell Broadbent moved to the crossbench after he lost Liberal Party preselection.

35 two more seats than Kim Beazley's: Labor won nineteen seats from the Coalition but lost one to the redistribution of electoral boundaries.

37 "I doubt": Tony Abbott, "Cultural self-confidence that is what is missing", *Proceedings of the Samuel Griffith Society*, vol. 28, 2016.

37 "In a classic case": John Howard, *A Sense of Balance*, HarperCollins, 2022, pp. 164–5.

39 a horror budget: William Bowe, "Budget polling, day two", *The Poll Bludger*, 5 April 2022.

40 Laura Tingle ... asked Chalmers: Interview with Laura Tingle, 7:30, ABC TV, 29 September 2022.

41 favoured men in suits: Treasury, "Advice on amending tax cuts to deliver broader cost-of-living relief", Australian Government, Canberra, 2024, https://treasury.gov.au/sites/default/files/2024-01/tax-cuts-treasury-advice.pdf.

42 "When faced with": Treasury, "Advice on amending tax cuts", p. 8.

44 "We're supporting taxpayers": Peter Dutton, 7:30, ABC TV, 7 February 2024.

45 "The truth is": Sir Robert Menzies, *The Measure of the Years*, Cassell Australia, 1970, p. 16.

46 "for a reform of this size": Jim Chalmers, *Glory Daze*, Melbourne University Press, 2013, p. 162.

49 "to do the right thing by Australians": Dr James O'Donnell, 2023 *Mapping Social Cohesion Report*, Scanlon Foundation, 2023.

53 almost a quarter of the global economy's modest growth: OEC, "G20 GDP growth – second quarter of 2024", OECD website, 12 September 2024, https://oecd.org/en/data/insights/statistical-releases/2024/09/g20-gdp-growth-second-quarter-2024.html.

55 Millennials born between 1981 and 1995: Just under half of those aged thirty to thirty-four owned their own home at the last census, taken in 2021, a post-war low for this group, and seventeen points behind the national home ownership rate of 67 per cent. The home ownership rate for baby boomers at the equivalent age in 1981 was 68 per cent, when the national home ownership rate was 70 per cent. Australian Institute of Health and Welfare, "Home ownership and housing tenure", AIHW website, 12 July 2024, https://aihw.gov.au/reports/australias-welfare/home-ownership-and-housing-tenure.

55–6 "However, the main beneficiary": Shaun Ratcliff, "Gen-Z are different: Explanations for the growing generational gap in Australian politics", Accent Research, November 2023.

56 The last census: Rounding explains the slightly higher rate for those with freehold title.

56 The landlord class: Australian Taxation Office, "Taxation statistics 2021–22", ATO website, 14 June 2024, https://ato.gov.au/about-ato/research-and-statistics/in-detail/taxation-statistics/taxation-statistics-2021-22.

56 post-war high of 71 per cent: See John Howard, *A Sense of Balance*, pages 206–7: "[The home ownership] rate in 1947 in Australia was 53.4 per cent, having been at or slightly below that figure before World War II. It rose sharply to a peak of 71.4 per cent in 1966, from which it has subsided to its current level (of 66.4 per cent in 2021)." He did not mention that the rate began falling on his watch.

57 "I'm sure": Albanese quoted in James Massola and James Crowe, "Negative gearing in Labor's sights as Albanese readies for election battle", 25 September 2024.

57 Some compared it: Annabel Crabb, "The prime minister's new beach house has just made his job – and his colleagues' – much harder", ABC News, 16 October 2024.

57 One in three members and senators: The taxation statistics show 4.2 per cent of taxpayers have at least two rental properties. I have rounded down that figure to remove the fraction who don't also own their own home. The figure for parliamentarians is taken from the ABC's search of the register of interests and may undercount the total because it does not include those MPs who operate trusts. Tom Crowley, Ahmed Yussuf, Mark Doman, Katia Shatoba and Thomas Brettell, "How many properties do Australian federal politicians own?" ABC News, 16 October 2024.

58 "The sense the [Morrison) Government": Loughnane and Hume, *Review of the 2022 Federal Election*.

59 "It's not just housing": Peter Dutton, 7:30, ABC TV, 16 May 2024.

60 "race for space": Brendan Coates, "Don't blame migrants for the housing crisis", *The Australian*, 22 May 2023.

60 "Construction is taking longer": National Housing Supply and Affordability Council, *State of the Housing System*, Australian Government, Canberra, 2024, https://nhsac.gov.au/sites/nhsac.gov.au/files/2024-05/state-of-the-housing-system-2024.pdf.

60 rate of growth: Australian Bureau of Statistics, "Labour force, Australia", ABS, 2024, https://abs.gov.au/statistics/labour/employment-and-unemployment/labour-force-australia/aug-2024#key-statistics.

60 new jobs have been split 50/50: Employment in health care and social assistance grew by 250,000, or 12.2 per cent – double the national average. Construction created 182,000 jobs (up 15.4 per cent) while electricity, gas and water added another 47,000 (up 28.6 per cent). These three sectors account for more than half of all the jobs created since the last election. See Australian Bureau of Statistics, "Industry, Occupation and Sector Quarterly (May) Table 04. Employed persons by Industry division of main job (ANZSIC) – Trend, seasonally adjusted, and original" in "Labour force, Australia, detailed", July 2024, ABS, https://abs.gov.au/statistics/labour/employment-and-unemployment/labour-force-australia-detailed/jul-2024.

62 "For many young people": Bill Kelty, "The Labor Party has lost its way", *Pearls and Irritations* (johnmenadue.com), 5 October 2024.

63 "the creator of our great party": See, for example, Peter Dutton to the Liberal Party (NSW Division) State Convention, "Standing up for the forgotten Australians", Menzies Research Centre, 1 December 2023.

63 "has 'a stake in the country'": "Chapter 1 – The Forgotten People", Menzies Virtual Museum, https://menziesvirtualmuseum.org.au/transcripts/the-forgotten-people/59-chapter-1-the-forgotten-people.

Correspondence

Thomas Keneally

What I like about Watson's mind is his capacity to connect the mytho-poetic to the political, and he can do it without hearing from him, generally, any grunt of effort. The Trump he gives us, essentially, is a special kind of Ogre, and is a fascinating figure in that the more politically literate people insult him with words like "autocratic," "authoritarian," "demagogue," "misogynist," the bigger he grows. Elegant abuse is his meat, his drink. This is why one can call Watson's essay charming, even if it is about the end of America and of all our traditional ties to America. And then, just as the poor old king dozes off in the midst of discussing the Ogre with the Townspeople, two apparently ordinary folk wander in, Harris and Walz, who somehow, by not having a lifetime of experience of politics, can find the words to diminish the Ogre. They were ordinary words, but they bring a previously unseen pallor to the Ogre's cheeks. "Weird" was one of these words. The people watched in wonder and hoped the code words would keep their power to make the Ogre smaller. But even those who rejoiced still have a curiosity about the Ogre. We would like to live for a day in a Trump-amended America just to see how fantastically bad it could be. Let's hope we never find out on a more permanent basis. For one thing, if Trump triumphs, imagine the foul mob of would-be Führers it will unleash in Australia. May the unutterable God save us!

The early United States was an experimental field in which the federation idea was tested. In 1787, the federal government had a limited palette of duties, the right to wage war and enter treaties, but not to raise taxes or maintain a federal army. A number of former revolutionaries in central and western Massachusetts, led by a well-connected American revolutionary officer named Daniel Shays, staged a rebellion. Faced with Massachusetts state taxes, and business favouritism, and a lack of currency, the minimalist federal government could do little but take note. Shays' Rebellion helped federalist leader Alexander Hamilton push for a stronger federal entity and a new constitution. But the question of how potent a federal government should be has been an abiding question for all federal nations since, and the idea of minimalist federal governments has an abiding appeal to many Americans, particularly a federation that doesn't tell you which guns you can't own. It soon became apparent that it didn't to Australians.

We expected a more interventionist strain in our state and federal politics in principle. I remember a time in California, where I taught some seasons of graduate writing. We used to go hiking on Sunday mornings in Modjeska Canyon, in the Santa Ana Mountains. Helena Modjeska was a famed Polish actress who settled in the canyon mouth about the same time as an ancestor of mine, John Keneally, West Australian–pardoned Fenian convict, added to Los Angeles' then 9000 non-indigenous inhabitants. In the restaurant at the canyon head, businessmen from L.A. parked their recreational bikes and ate breakfast at a diner, and posted stickers about the arrogant overreach of the Californian government, which was then legislating to make bike helmets compulsory for citizen-bikers. To an Australian they seemed to be insisting on their right to suffer a cerebral haemorrhage or fractured neck. But what they were protesting about was an overactive Californian legislature's right to pass such intrusive legislation. Those men, now aged if not deceased, would also believe it is not the state or federal government's right to intrude in commerce or to order you to take a Covid vaccination, and would look forward to the appropriately libertarian President Trump for a remake of the system.

Ideas and administrative solutions that have worked in Australia without comment or civic resistance, but that would arouse immediate rebellion in the United States, include the compulsory tuberculosis X-ray system put in place to eliminate TB in my youth, and seatbelt regulation. If a regulation (helmet-wearing, for example) makes patent practical sense to an Australian populace, no philosophical or libertarian resistance to a government's right to pass such laws will be raised, or if raised will be a highly minority view. To explain the operations of a government–funded and devised body like the Australian Electoral Commission, especially given its statutory independence, to say such a body would have saved toxic lies and accusations in US politics, does no good. The Electoral Commission would still look like "federal tyranny" to a right-wing American voter. Its website claims, "The AEC is not the arbiter of truth regarding political communication, and do[es] not seek to censor debate in any way. However, when it comes to the election process we conduct, we're the experts and we're active in defending Australian democracy." Such a banal observation, accepted with a "Tell us something we don't know" by Australians, would cause outrage in many American breasts. A federal, central body running elections! Nightmare on Pennsylvania Avenue!

The federal government gun buy-back was, to Americans, another excessive and barely believable exercise of power by the Howard government. Southerners asked me occasionally about that "socialist goddam tyrant John Howard." For that matter, the fact our constitution was an act of the British Parliament, midwifed into existence by a fascinating set of Australian commissioners named Deakin (Victoria), Kingston (South Australia) and Barton (aka Tosspot Toby, New South Wales), has no place in Australian mythology. Their brave work, by the way, persuading the British to accept the constitution as voted for in a six-state plebiscite, is a great story of our constitutional development, but as for all things constitutional in Australia, it barely raises a flicker of enthusiasm in a country in which the teaching of civics is minimal. "Socialism without ideas" again, to quote a nineteenth-century visitor to Australia, and as for our medical system ... A few years past I landed in a Wildcat on the USS *Kitty Hawk*, the normal 1.5-second carrier landing for an aircraft. And at a Coke and fruit juice cocktail party aboard, I spoke with the aircraft carrier's chief physician and dental surgeon. They frowned when I introduced myself as the brother of a physician, Johnny, at Westmead Children's. They said they'd been helicoptered there for a visit and then took me by the elbow and broke to me in a frowning, "Oh Brother, Where Art Thou?" manner, "Your hospitals are very socialist."

I was tempted to say, "Without ideas." But it would have been unworthy of their demeanour, which was that of warning a friendly foreigner that his institutions were imperilled and his house on fire. But what was apparent to them as political heresy was to us the desired nature of things. I have never heard any conservative candidate for Australian office attack public health on the grounds it was too socialist. I have heard candidates and citizens of all stripes attack it for long waiting times in emergency departments: that is, for not being socialist enough.

In America, democracy is designed county up, whereas our constitution has a quality, reinforced by history, of Commonwealth down. Hence, there are differences in our voting papers, given that the presidential voting booklet is the work of a specific county and may contain, as well as the presidential ballot, the voting form for a state-based judge, for a state referendum on perhaps the sale of fur, and for the election of a county police chief.

The Founding Fathers of the United States, if anything, put an authoritarian spin on their constitution with the Electoral College. The college seems to be a filter of political conservatism designed possibly to correct the popular vote. The number of each state's Electoral College members varies by population, California being top with fifty-four, Texas having forty, New York twenty-eight, and at the bottom six states (Delaware, North Dakota, South Dakota, Alaska, Vermont and

Wyoming) and the District of Columbia have three each. In the middle, Michigan and Georgia have fifteen and sixteen respectively.

Federal officeholders like senators and members of the House of Representatives cannot be appointed. There have been more motions to amend the Electoral College than any other aspect of the constitution. The state *appoints*, not elects, members of the College, which the National Archives calls "a process not a location." The state sends a certificate of the College Vote to Washington. Most states now have an arrangement that awards the winner of the popular poll the presidency, but it was not so always. Did the grand democracy once so favour appointees over the elected that they could let them potentially negate the popular vote? It's on 6 January that the vice president presents the vote of the Electoral College, generally as a matter of course, and a combined Congressional session finally counts them and formally confirms the winner. And, as we know, to disrupt that in 2021 Trump's minions attacked the Capitol! Mike Pence saved the constitution by turning up for the procedure. Trump's millions cursed him for it. For it has become glamorous for them to abuse the constitution. Abusing the Australian meat-an'-spuds constitution breeds no enthusiasm in Australians because we must find that rare phenomenon first. This fantastically successful documents when read, has at first, as I once said, "All the charm and drama of the Dee Why Bowls Club Articles of Association." The committee wrote to me to assert that their articles of association had a drama and a pulse superior to the constitution's. In any case, sufficient to say there will be millions of voters in this presidential election who wish harm to the US constitution.

I believe those who have lost hope have done so under the sting and inhumanity and the totalitarian – yes, hold your hats, kids! – tyranny of our economic beliefs. If any system permits of a dictatorial and authoritarian view of the world and reduces the activity of humanity to one overall and limited mode of being, then neoliberal market economics and the "trickle-down" myth is it. First, the citizen is reduced to a mere consumer: not the amalgam of impulses that a real citizen is, but a mere customer. In maximising the market, unions have no place and the market itself will devise rewards. Doubt about economic process has no place, and government's place is to get the hell out of the way and reduce red tape and taxes on the creativeness of business. As Richard Denniss of the Australia Institute argues, Australian business has accepted "the good bits" of trickle-down economics, but not the strict theory that the market is self-sustaining, and therefore there should not need to be paid billions in bounties to continue plundering the place. For while the humble should not be cosseted with handouts, and while the middle and working classes must bear the burden of fixing the economy by selling their investments cheap, corporations must be bailed out, because they're just too bloody big to live without! We have market-alienated folk in Australia and their voices were heard in the last election, as minor as have been the mousy displays of intent in the matter from the Labor government.

If let to operate freely, goes the doctrine, the market will send its riches down the chain, and any attempts by government to intrude with welfare, such as spending on public health, which undermines health not as a birthright but as the good market it is, delays the holy day when the market will at last lift all boats and equalise all tides. The market's totalitarian economics of trickle-down, and the adherence of the market and the Congress to it, has been attacked by Bernie Sanders, as Watson tells us. Biden, who has sometimes spoken like an old Labor leader and whom Watson argues is one of the more notable of presidents, while not treading fully the path of a New Deal that might reconcile America to itself, has passed much legislation of the service-of-humanity type.

The worst thing was that under the orthodoxy of trickle-down, everything was a business, even marriage. If you want to hear the lash of totalitarianism's deathly tongue, listen to the definition of marriage of one of its high priests. Gary Becker of the Chicago School of Economics received a Nobel Prize for achieving economic definitions of marriage, drug addiction, racism and the Rotten Kid Syndrome (the spoiled and rebellious child of the honest capitalist). Marriage, he says, is "a calculable transaction between two utility maximising agents," in which "love as default was a non-marketable commodity." Shakespeare specifically pre-gave the remedy for such a miserable view: "For thy sweet love, remembered, such wealth brings / That then I scorn to change my state with Kings." And I swear on the grounds of transcendence that when Shakespeare says "such wealth brings," he's not talking about the state of the market.

The Trump supporters want to see the constitution come to ruin because it is seen as essentially linked to this toxic economics, an idea which American corporations are pleased to push. Indeed, it is very American, given the Calvinist tradition of prefigured redemption or predestination can be pressed into service to depict the market not only as a force in its own right, but as the will of God. But the constitution is not the market. Neoliberalism was a con job to close down America's manufacturing and send its jobs offshore. Another part of the con job was the privatisation of public schools to make them Charter Schools, one of which I have visited on Chicago's South Side. They are staffed by non-union teachers doing their best in huge education mills in poor neighbourhoods. Within these market-driven schools, which have all the multi-thousand charm of a battery chicken farm, a corporation using the state's budget, by its economies, joylessly educates some thousands of young Americans, mainly Hispanic and African, for a future as gangbangers or military personnel, wedded to the armed forces for medical coverage. We don't have them here, though Dr Brendan Nelson, while Minister of Education for five years, spoke warmly of the concept, omitting the fact that given these schools were low-grade education farms, a Chicago police post of several cops, equipped for everything from shoot-outs to riots, lies in the decaying front hall of what was once built to be a mechanism of equality.

Whenever you exploit schools or universities or aged homes as mere businesses, and the human pilgrims within as mere consumers, you ignite a rage among the victims. Welcome "Robodebt," a machine of despair and helpless rage!

Biden has already attacked this idea by many of his policies, but raw market economics is the abiding dogma of the age. And it is not complex – though, listening to Becker's definitions of social phenomena, you would think it was. Under the name "political economy," it was the thinking behind the Irish Famine, where politicians proposed that feeding the starving must not create dependence in the Irish masses since that would undermine the grain market, and the market must not be undermined. For the market, greed-on-wheels, is not only the great Good. It is the Great God.

We ask if any of this was the nature of the rage that took over the Capitol on 6 January 2021? Is Trump, ultimate businessman, now simply selling their fury back to the misused and rebellious for a neat and astounding profit? Will the market ever permit the American infrastructure to be rebuilt by the – gasp, and cover the children's ears! – *government*? Public and private sitting down together like William Blake's lion and lamb?

Revolutionaries never have behaved with reason and moderation in response to official barbarism. If Kamala Harris has the gifts of reason to undermine Trump for now, does she have the gifts to defeat neoliberalism, and to bring the Proud Boys, the Rise Above Nation and QAnon back into America?

Thomas Keneally

Emma Shortis

I recorded a podcast episode with Don not long after his essay was published. We spoke at length about what the Democrats under Harris had to offer the American people, and whether it would be enough to convince them to turn out for her. Or at least enough of them, in enough of the right places. We both worry that Harris doesn't have the answers people are looking for; or, put another way, that the Harris/Walz ticket doesn't appear to recognise that part of what explains the plateauing of enthusiasm for Harris must surely be the Democratic Party's inability to reconcile what Don describes as its "progressive pragmatism" with decades of mostly whole-hearted embrace of a neoliberal agenda. That it simply cannot bridge, as Don puts it, "the disconnect between mainstream politics and the reality of life for millions."

Part of the answer, as Don writes, is for Democrats to be honest; to own the mistakes of the past. That must involve a basic level of authenticity; something the Harris/Walz ticket appeared to offer, at least initially. At the Democratic National Convention in August, in what was then her most important speech to date, Harris avoided, exactly as Don suggested, "the debilitating habits of American speechmaking that undermine authenticity by seeking it in tattered clichés of the 'only in America could someone like me be president' kind."

After I finished recording with Don, I went back online to check in on the campaign; Harris had just finished a televised "live rally" event with Oprah Winfrey. It was a typically slick production. Oprah was joined by such celebrities as Jennifer Lopez, Meryl Streep, Julia Roberts and Chris Rock. She spoke to grassroots organisers and, once Harris joined her on the set, to the family of a young woman who had died as a direct result of draconian abortion laws in the wake of the overturning of *Roe v. Wade*. It was, by all accounts, a triumph.

As she introduced the vice president, Oprah said: "in no other country on this Earth could her story unfold the way it has."

Don Watson captures the bizarre, Hollywood unreality of the United States like no one else.

Trump, as he does with everything, magnifies the effect. Earlier this year, I somehow found myself at a Trump rally. Well, a rally of sorts – Trump was speaking at the Libertarian Convention in Washington, D.C. attempting to hold together his loose coalition of right-wingers and anti-war libertarians. I was there partly to support the Julian Assange campaign, which had long found support from those libertarians. They were pressuring Trump to commit to pardoning Assange, as Robert F. Kennedy Jr and Trump surrogate Vivek Ramaswamy had done. They were unsuccessful – later, when Trump picked J.D. Vance as his running mate, it became clear that the libertarians had lost their internal ideological war against the much more national-security-friendly far right. The "wolves in MAGA hats," as Assange himself later described them, don't want to dismantle the deep state – they want to control it.

Even in these somewhat unusual circumstances – much of the libertarian crowd heckled and booed Trump, contemptuous of his unfulfilled promise to take on the "deep state," and deeply opposed to Covid-era stimulus and vaccine mandates – being at a Trump event is a kind of out-of-body experience. It's like being inside a screen. Time moves in fits and starts. The light is strange.

As the crowd waited – and, in this case, as the simmering tensions between Libertarian Party delegates and shipped-in Trump supporters over seating almost boiled over – the Trump playlist blared through the speakers. I did a live cross to Channel 7's breakfast program as "Memories" from the musical *Cats* played in the background. It was, in every sense, surreal. Tim Walz is right. It is weird.

Weird and, for an outsider, inescapably scary. You can feel it, sitting just underneath *Cats* and the Mamas & the Papas and Metallica and even, inexplicably, Rufus Wainwright's rendition of Leonard Cohen's "Hallelujah" (the "height of blasphemy," as Wainwright later posted on Instagram) – the bubbling violence.

It is at once terrifying while not feeling real at all. It's so easy to imagine it happening, just as Don sees and does not see a man being shot on the streets of New York. I can imagine someone getting shot as "Memories" blasts from the speakers, as the libertarians and the wolves in red hats fight it out over the seats closest to the stage. I can see what the pictures will look like, hear the cable news commentary, and yet I am unable to believe, really believe, that it will happen while I, specifically, am there.

That's the only way to reconcile the risk of going. To set it aside, to reassure yourself that it's safe and they aren't that different.

And they aren't that different, not really. But also, they are.

And they are *like that*, as Don worries. They have always been like that.

So why, as Don asks, do we watch?

We are all, surely, transfixed by the spectacle. It's hard *not* to watch, even if through half-closed eyes, head angled slightly away from the screen, as the former and maybe future president of the United States sways on a stage to "Ave Maria," "Nothing Compares 2 U" and "Memories."

Trump's playlist tells you so much about him. He is incoherent, incurious about actual meaning, has attention that is so easily grabbed and yet is impossible to keep. The leaps between the songs give you whiplash. Experiencing it in person was genuinely upsetting. As in his stump speeches, there is no beginning, middle or end. Nothing to hold on to.

But the spectacle isn't what keeps us there; the spectacle alone could not hold our transfixed attention for so long (surely?). It's too exhausting, too stupid. We watch, surely, for other reasons. Because we know, instinctively, how much this all matters to us, too.

Australia's relationship with the United States is, we are so often told, above petty domestic politics. It is above presidents and prime ministers. It sits instead at the core of our nationhoods. Domestic politics is irrelevant.

Donald Trump is, in many ways, a truth-teller. Or a truth-revealer. There are no clean dividing lines between domestic politics and the United States' role in the world. Australia's alliance with the United States is not above domestic politics. It is inextricably connected to it.

The projection of the American spectacle outwards has significant implications for the rest of us. That's true for obvious reasons, a list often repeated: how a Harris or Trump administration manages its relationship with China, how big the tariffs are and how US monetary policy changes, or doesn't, will all have huge impacts on the global economy and our own. How either approaches NATO and Ukraine. How either manages the United States' relationships with Israel and Iran.

Donald Trump isn't an isolationist. He does view American power differently to Biden and Harris. And to Dick Cheney. But he doesn't abhor violence. He loves it. One of the things Don Watson captures about him so startlingly – one of the insights in this essay that dawns on you weeks later, in the middle of the night – is Trump's evolutionary arc from WWE to UFC – from World Wrestling Entertainment to the Ultimate Fighting Championship.

The violence of American politics was never pretend. They've just stopped pretending it is.

And "the real tests," as Don writes, "are yet to come." After reading Don's essay, it becomes harder to imagine good outcomes for the United States in November, and after. None of this goes away if Harris does pull it off – and that's a very big "if." And in any case, can Harris win by enough to create a clean break, to find enough space? Probably not, and especially not if she can't win Congress.

What does this mean for the rest of us? What does it mean for our politics? A headline in *The Guardian*, published in the week I wrote this, reads: "South Australia's upper house narrowly rejects 'Trumpian' bill to wind back abortion care." They're trying it on in Queensland, too.

Even in the (relatively) good scenario, there are ramifications for our domestic future. What "lessons" will the Australian Labor Party draw from a Democratic victory? That progressive policies drive voter support in key demographics left-leaning parties need to win? Or that you need only chase the swing voters, and to get them you need to court the Cheneys?

And what if we have to face a real-real test? What if they *are* like that? What if American democracy is an empty shell?

What are our responsibilities if our very best friend in the world uses the National Guard or the military against "enemies within"? Should we say something? Would we do anything differently?

Or would we just keep watching?

Emma Shortis

Correspondence

David Smith

I lived in Michigan from 2004 to 2010, and I was delighted by Don Watson's descriptions of it in *High Noon*. He captured the vibrancy of Kalamazoo, a city barely known to most Americans except for its unusual name. I winced with recognition at his description of Ann Arbor's Kerrytown market, whose "ageing boomers sold the stuff they've been selling in such markets for half a century." That hasn't changed since I lived there. It's worth dwelling a bit on Watson's account of Detroit, because it played a critical role in the 2020 election and may again in 2024. When I first saw it, twenty years ago, I was shocked when I realised that its skyscrapers, which looked so impressive from a distance, were mostly empty, and had been for a long time. Some had trees growing inside them, or on their roofs. The city has changed a lot since then.

Watson notes the role of Quicken Loans founder Dan Gilbert in refurbishing downtown Detroit. He describes Gilbert as the city's "modern benefactor," a "financial genius" and "generous giver to good causes," a "social visionary and founder and the proprietor of a company consistently ranked in the top thirty 'best companies to work for.'" All that is true. But in 2010, the year he moved Quicken's headquarters to Detroit, he was known mainly to the city as the majority owner of the Cleveland Cavaliers, LeBron James's NBA team and an annual playoff rival of the Detroit Pistons. Gilbert became nationally famous that year for his unhinged response to James's announcement that he was leaving Cleveland for the Miami Heat. In a furious open letter posted to the Cavaliers' website and addressed to their fans in northeast Ohio, Gilbert denounced the "narcissistic," "cowardly betrayal" of "our former hero, who grew up in the very region he deserted this evening." He personally guaranteed (in all caps) that the Cavaliers would win an NBA championship before James did: "You can take it to the bank." The Cavaliers didn't win a championship until James graciously returned to Cleveland a few years later, having won two in Miami.

I can't fully convey the madness of this letter, which was erratically punctuated and written in Comic Sans (Gilbert's staff told *The Wall Street Journal* that he uses the font in all his communications). But it says a lot about the kinds of figures who get proclaimed as saviours of places marked by chronic institutional decay. They need not just money but titanic self-belief and minimal self-consciousness. They flourish in locations so hollowed out that anyone with a big enough sales pitch will be flung the keys in desperation. Whether they turn out to be frauds or visionaries often depends on timing. Gilbert returned to Detroit at the right time, when the city was going bankrupt and reeling from the embarrassment of Mayor Kwame Kilpatrick, who was sentenced to twenty-eight years in prison on federal corruption convictions. Mayoral replacement Dave Bing, a mostly powerless Detroit Pistons legend backed by Gilbert, described his job as "to knock down as many barriers as possible and get out of the way." Gilbert bought up more than ninety-five buildings in downtown Detroit and employed a private security force to protect them, which provided a welcome measure of safety but also a lack of accountability. The 4000 (mostly white) employees he brought to the city helped revitalise a place that had been losing population for generations, but also put upward pressure on rents.

Gilbert and others have helped downtown Detroit move past the "ruin porn" phase of its existence. When I was last there in 2015, I was told the city's police were deterring visitors from taking photos of Michigan Central Station, an abandoned Beaux-Arts tower surrounded by tall grass. Detroit, the police would explain, was still a city with people living in it, and they didn't appreciate tourists treating it like Pompeii. The former railway station, closed since 1988, was about to be renovated by another of the powerful figures Watson names, Matty Moroun. In case any readers did a double take at Watson's mention that the Moroun family owns the Ambassador Bridge connecting the United States and Canada: yes, in America such a crucial piece of infrastructure can be privately owned by a single individual or family. The Ambassador Bridge accounts for 25 per cent of trade between the two countries, who are each other's largest trading partners. It is the busiest international crossing in North America. And the Morouns, as Watson says, "have done all they can to prevent the construction of a new bridge that would compete with theirs." The repair of Michigan Central, close by his bridge, was Matty Moroun's big contribution to civic life in Detroit. In 2018 he sold it to Ford Motors, who have since reopened it as a "technology and artistic hub."

Moroun had too much of a reputation as a "slum landlord," in Watson's words, ever to be regarded as a benevolent figure in Detroit. Nor did he try very hard to be seen as one. The Fords are another story. Since the beginning of the twentieth century they have been recognised both as benefactors and owners of southeast Michigan. Watson nicely captures the contradictions of Ford's dominion. In 1932, the same year Henry Ford's private security force killed striking workers at the Rouge River Plant, his son Edsel commissioned the Mexican communist painter Diego Rivera to memorialise Ford's assembly line in a series of murals. The murals are worth seeing, as is the Detroit Institute of Arts that houses them. The Ford family's name and legacy are everywhere in downtown Detroit, from the century-old Henry Ford Hospital to Ford Field, the football stadium that hosts the Detroit Lions. The Ford Foundation is the second-largest philanthropic foundation in the country. Ford Motors, however, has been known in the twenty-first century for shifting production of its vehicles to places like Mexico and China, continuing the process widely blamed for Detroit's decline since the 1960s.

What kind of city emerges from the vast wealth and ambiguous motives of figures like Gilbert, Moroun and the Fords? Most of their monuments are confined to a stretch from downtown to midtown, just a few square miles of a city that is physically bigger than Manhattan, Boston and San Francisco combined. Beyond that, Watson writes, are "streets lined with long-empty, collapsing, weed-infested houses." Of course, there are still hundreds of thousands of people in the city, but it used to house two million, and large parts of it seem deserted. Even the refurbished downtown, Watson recounts, feels "plain empty" of people. However much Detroit has been improved, no one who can remember its heyday would say it has been "fixed." Watson writes: "If you want to know America, know Detroit. If you want to fix America, fix Detroit." Many Americans who don't share Watson's politics would agree.

Donald Trump talks about American cities as unmitigated nightmares. The violence, crime and corruption he so often invokes in his speeches are usually in reference to cities like Detroit, Chicago and Washington, understood by his audience as places that are mostly Black and run by Democrats. The fixes Trump proposes for these cities are simple and appealing for his base, few of whom live in them. Get rid of "corrupt" local governments, put them in the hands of federal administrators, and send in the military to clean them up. Or, as he said recently, give city police forces (friendly figures in Trump cosmology, criminally hobbled by liberal authorities) "one really violent day" to do their jobs. Republicans view cities like Detroit (majority Black), Milwaukee, Philadelphia and Atlanta (plurality Black) and Phoenix (plurality Latino) with immense suspicion at election time. In swing states that otherwise have large white majorities, election outcomes may be finally determined in these majority-minority cities, whose vote tallies usually come in last because of the logistical operations involved in counting them.

Even before Trump, Michigan Republicans would tell stories of how Detroit officials supposedly wait to see how many votes Democrats need to win statewide, then come up with them. It's a myth with no basis in evidence or reality, but it makes sense to white conservatives who see Detroit as a lawless hellhole with the power to corrupt the whole country. During the 2020 election, hundreds of suburbanites descended on Detroit's Cobo Center, where the city's votes were being counted. Untrained Republican "poll watchers" protested the results before they even knew what the results were. They observed routine events, like ballots being moved from one table to another, and cried foul, demanding explanations from harried election officials. This was one of the reasons the vote count took so long. It was also one of the reasons courts were flooded after the election with thousands of pages of affidavits that contained exactly no evidence of electoral fraud.

You might think suspicions like these could be alleviated by an Australian-style, centralised, independent election authority, rather than leaving the running of elections and the counting of votes to partisan state and local authorities. But Republicans have fiercely resisted any federalisation of election law, probably because they benefit from the status quo, which gives them control of electoral rules and districting in the majority of states. As it happened, a quirk of Michigan law could have upended the entire 2020 election.

In Michigan, every county appoints a board of two Republicans and two Democrats to certify results, regardless of the partisan composition of the county. Sixty-eight per cent of voters in Wayne County voted for Joe Biden in 2020, including almost 95 per cent in Detroit, the county seat. But for a few hours in mid-November, the county's two Republican board members refused to certify the results, citing minor mismatches in precinct rolls affecting fewer than 100 votes out of 800,000. Even these glitches were not evidence of fraud, but administrative errors that had no bearing on the legality of the votes. One of the Republicans said she would be willing to certify results in neighbouring suburbs like Livonia (which are majority white), but not in Detroit. Eventually both members relented as protesters gathered outside the board meeting.

This spectacle, which earned a celebratory tweet from Trump, was enough to cause trouble further up the line. The certification of Michigan's statewide results is also the responsibility of a four-member bipartisan board. In the days leading up to certification, one of the Republicans indicated he would not certify the results because of the problem in Wayne County and other rumoured irregularities throughout the state. It was left to the other Republican board member, a forty-year-old lawyer named Aaron van Langevelde, to side with the board's Democrats and certify the results, ending a debacle that could have reinvigorated efforts to overthrow the election in other states. Biden won Michigan by about 154,000 votes. In Detroit he got almost 241,000 to Trump's nearly 13,000. While Trump lost the state he had won four years previously, he almost doubled his 2016 vote in Detroit on the strength of voters like Solomon, the "hardworking Black man" who told Watson he was lucky to live in a country with Sky News.

The Trump campaign has hopes of making serious inroads with Black men this year. If he can do it, Trump is likely to win. No Democrat since Lyndon Johnson has won a majority of white votes at a presidential election, and Democrats rely on overwhelming margins of Black voters to get them over the line. But if Trump loses, it may be because his campaign directed too few resources in states like Michigan to getting Black voters out for him, and too many towards trying to disqualify their votes.

David Smith

Bruce Wolpe

If you want to read the truth on American politics, read Don Watson. It's not just that a most engaging, far-reaching and penetrating mind pores over the landscape of America, it's the distilled wisdom he brings from immersion in politics and culture over several decades, imbued with a love of language and words and elegiac style. Don reveals, discerns and grapples with the truth of what is happening in the United States as it stands on the brink.

In 2016, it was Don, in Wisconsin, who saw and understood Trump's emergence and the power of his message, especially to the white working class in America. They were the alienated, the disaffected, the cheated. They struck back at the empire.

The country did not go completely nuts. Hillary Clinton won the popular vote by three million. But the Founding Fathers did not trust the people in 1787 as they wrote the constitution. The Electoral College was created, and ensured that at times the overall popular will could – and should – be thwarted by the undemocratic exercise of voting power by smaller states, which had inordinate representation as presidential election votes were counted. When the republic was established, the founders ensured the smaller agrarian states had a bigger proportional voice. The founders also gave the Senate the same unbalanced structure, so that Wyoming's two senators have the same power as California's two senators.

Trump is a singular character, almost unique. Ronald Reagan had a lot of Hollywood wattage, Kennedy and Obama had immense charisma. Trump excels in spectacle. For seventeen seasons on television, Trump was on air weekly as the CEO-in-chief, and his audience of tens of millions were comfortable with him when he stepped onto the presidential stage. As Don writes, "Trump has turned Republican politics, and therefore much of American politics, into the wildly adversarial and addictive world of TV wrestling, an entertainment he used to make money and forge his public persona." Until Trump leaves the stage, he owns the stage.

Trump tapped into the resentments felt by those Hillary Clinton termed "the deplorables." The elites, Don writes, "In the name of free trade and globalisation … sold out their jobs and left their communities in ruin; then they told them how to think and what they could and could not say … And a Black man and his Black wife were in the White House."

If Harris loses this election, it will be because that America was not ready for her, eight years after the Obamas left the White House, and four years after Biden defeated Trump. The polls do not capture this resentment. Maybe it will not determine the outcome. We will only know in the days after the election.

On Trump's rallies – the core element to his success – Don accounts for their power:

> Everyone saw the mass rallies and the strutting, pouting histrionics; the scapegoating of migrant; the xenophobia and barely disguised racism … his cultivation of popular fantasies of grievance, betrayal, plots and conspiracies, his self-portrayal as the great leader who alone could rid Americans – real Americans – of oppressive elites … the bullying regard for strength … and of course the endless lies. Some commentators used the word "autocratic." Some said "authoritarian." Very few were prepared to say "fascist."

It's the lies. Never before have we seen and heard so many – not just untruths – but outright lies. Told with reckless abandon. And when the lies are called out, the lies are repeated. Bob Woodward, in his new book, *War*, confirms Watson's judgement. General Mark Milley, the former chairman of the Joint Chiefs of Staff, told Woodward that Trump is "fascist to the core" and "the most dangerous man in America."

There is no shame anymore in American politics. Trump and his vice-presidential running mate, J.D. Vance, can make up lies about "illegal Haitian immigrants" eating the cats and dogs in Springfield, Ohio. It does not matter that the staunchly conservative *Republican* governor of Ohio, Mike DeWine, writes in *The New York Times*, "As a supporter of former President Donald Trump and Senator JD Vance, I am saddened by how they and others continue to repeat claims that lack evidence and disparage the legal migrants living in Springfield. This rhetoric hurts the city and its people, and it hurts those who have spent their lives there."

Trump is lying about this state and the good people, including the Haitian immigrants, in it – but DeWine is still going to vote for him.

In October, Trump returned to Butler, Pennsylvania, where he was shot by an assassin. "Those who want to stop us … have slandered me, impeached me, indicted me, tried to throw me off the ballot, and who knows, maybe even tried to kill me," Trump said. Just in case anyone missed what Trump was saying, his son Eric nailed it. "They tried to take away someone we all love," he said. "They tried to smear us. They came after us. They impeached him twice. And then, guys, they tried to kill him. They tried to kill him."

When those seeking power prevail and lie to cement their power, yes, that is fascism.

There is a brief reference in Don's piece to whether the United States faces a civil war. Especially if Trump loses, there will be acts of rebellion, insurrection, assault and upheaval. Violence has plagued the United States since the Revolution. In recent history, there was horrific domestic terrorism: the car bombing of a federal government building in Oklahoma in 1995. In 1993, eighty members of the Branch Davidians cult died in battle with the FBI in Waco, Texas. The 6 January 2021 assault on the Capitol and the peaceful transfer of power was a nation-shaking shock.

But a real civil war in the United States would be when several states declare they do not want to continue with the Union and move to secede. We are nowhere near this happening in America. If this question is of interest, please do read Jon Meacham's 2022 book on Abraham Lincoln, *And There Was Light: Abraham Lincoln and the American struggle*. What is occurring in the United States is not even close to the forces that brought on the Civil War in 1861.

Don also understands the power of Taylor Swift (and let's not forget Bruce and Oprah and Clooney, and Spike Lee and DeNiro). Don was on to something smart when he counselled, "Trump does not want to offend such a powerful woman. Deep down he surely knows she won't come his way, but perhaps he can persuade her to stay neutral." But Trump does not believe in neutral. You are either with him or he will try to destroy you. "I HATE TAYLOR SWIFT," he wrote on Truth Social after her Harris treason. What business leader in his or her right mind would publicly attack Taylor Swift? Trump posted the same judgement of Springsteen.

When he was defeated by Biden, and after the desecration of the Capitol on 6 January 2021, Trump was supposed to go away. But he didn't. Trump would not cede the field. His sense of personal grievance was too deep, too resonant, simply to walk away. He wanted vengeance and retribution and was – and is today – determined to get it. Trump wanted – needed – to return to power after being thwarted in the rigged, stolen 2020 election. He despatched Ron DeSantis, the Florida governor who was to be the non-Trump Trump without the baggage, from the Republican field for 2024, and then monstered those still standing, from Tim Scott to Doug Burgum to Nikki Haley.

Biden could not complete his mission of finally defeating Trump once and for all. Trump dogged him. By early June 2024, Trump was leading Biden in all the national polls and in virtually all the swing states that would decide the election. Biden saw it differently. Don writes that, "in May 2024 Joe Biden had reason to think his credentials were singular and beyond dispute, his great mission at least halfway to completion." But Biden did not command the arena. That was proven in his debate with Trump in June. It was a catastrophe. It was already clear to most Americans that Biden could not and should not serve a second term. Don reports, "Biden's smile is still there but the light has gone out of it. It doesn't carry. It doesn't flash. Age is making it rictus." It finally became clear to Democrats that there was no path to victory for him – that Biden would not win enough states to win the presidency.

The first assassination attempt made Trump a living martyr. The Republican convention just days later was the coronation of the saviour.

Biden was forced to step aside. Harris took the stage. The Democratic Party united behind her.

Can – will – Harris beat Trump? Don did not know the answer to that question at the end of August. I do not know the answer to that question in mid-October. "For Democrats, Trump's performance sharpens the pain … He looks so beatable … If only the Democrats had a candidate who could reliably make the case."

Watson finds Harris "compelling." So do tens and tens of millions of American voters. We will only know in November if she was compelling enough.

Bruce Wolpe

HIGH NOON

Correspondence

Paul Kane

In his unsettling essay "Circles," Ralph Waldo Emerson apprises us that "The field cannot be well seen from within the field." When that field is the expanse of American culture and politics, there's a lot to be said for the adroit outsider's perspective. The Frenchman Alexis de Tocqueville is perhaps the best example, whose *Democracy in America* (1835) still seems an accurate anatomy and, for some, a prescient warning about the dangers of "soft despotism," which "does not tyrannize, but compresses, enervates, extinguishes, and stupefies a people." Don Watson, with his 2001 Quarterly Essay, *Rabbit Syndrome*, and his monograph *American Journeys* (2008), proves to be – like de Tocqueville – just the sort of gimlet-eyed commentator who can see the field for what it is. This is equally evident in the new essay, though, unlike his aristocratic predecessor, Watson is more concerned with the prospect of hard despotism. In this, of course, he is not alone. When a quarter of Republicans think Donald Trump should seize power even if he loses the election, and when he himself declares he will be a dictator *only* on "day one," not only is there cause for concern, but one has to be a little puzzled as to why people haven't taken to the streets (already?) to decry the authoritarianism threatening American democracy. As Watson points out, Trump "is deliberately entering fascist territory, and it is surely stupid to ignore the signs he's sending." But then fascism and demagoguery are not unknown to the Republic.

*

> "I will do those things. So help me God. I shall live in your will and your right. And if any man tries to stop me in the fulfilling of that right and that will I'll break him. I'll break him like that!" He spread his arms far apart, shoulder-high, and crashed the right hand into the left palm. "Like that! I'll smite him. Hip and thigh, shinbone and

> neckbone, kidney punch, rabbit punch, uppercut, and solar plexus. And I don't care what I hit him with. Or how!"

So says Willie Stark, the protagonist of Robert Penn Warren's classic *All the King's Men* (1946). The crowd roars. Willie silences them with a gesture and then intones, "Your will is my strength." And, "Your need is my justice." (Compare Trump's "I am your retribution.") Warren's novel is loosely based on the life of Huey Long, the powerful corrupt governor of Louisiana and later senator, whose presidential ambitions to unseat Franklin Roosevelt in 1935 ended with an assassin's single bullet. Long was unusual for being a fascist of the left, a ruthless populist who transformed a decidedly backward state for the better, despite impeachments and indictments. FDR feared him more than Father Charles Coughlin, an antisemitic and nativist demagogue whose weekly radio broadcasts were followed by thirty million listeners, a quarter of the population. A supporter of Huey Long in the United States, and of Nazism and fascism abroad, he was finally silenced by the Catholic Church. Woody Guthrie put it best: "yonder comes Father Coughlin wearin' the silver chain / Cash in his stomach and Hitler on the brain."

Demagogues were much on the minds of the Founding Fathers, who had read their Plato ("tyranny naturally arises out of democracy") and ancient history (especially Polybius) and were, accordingly, deeply ambivalent about democracy and its prospects. It's why they devised that bane of American politics the Electoral College as a compromise with the Southern slave states but also as a way to ensure representative rather than direct democracy. Mob rule is what they feared. Electors were to be upright men of independent judgement, insulated from the tumult and disorder of factionalism. It's a maddening irony now that the Electoral College is what allows for minority rule in the US, paving the way for undemocratic authoritarianism, as Trump probably cannot (and certainly did not twice previously) win the popular vote. (Five US presidents have won election while losing the popular vote.) For all its attempts to thwart demagoguery by limiting the franchise and shielding electors, the US Constitution has managed to facilitate it. In fact, it didn't take long for this demagogic flaw (among other flaws) to become obvious.

As early as 1795, a fiery and foppish Dr Michael Leib from Philadelphia was convincing poor German immigrants of his tender concern for them, going eventually from the State House to the US Congress by means of his political machine, the German Republican Society. Increasingly, as states dropped property qualifications for voting, the old guard decried demagogues everywhere, until, by the Jacksonian period of the 1830s, politics had begun to resemble a shabby circus, albeit at times a very nasty one in the lead-up to the Civil War. The political polarisation that pro-slavery and anti-slavery forces generated continued into the

Reconstruction period, especially in the 1870s with the rise of the Ku Klux Klan and, conversely, the "bloody shirt" demagogues who whipped up latent hatred and resentment of the South as a way to deflect criticism of their own glaring failures. And so on, and so on, into the twentieth century and up to the present. *Plus ça change, plus c'est la même chose?* So what's different this time around?

*

In England, in 1826, the Utilitarian philosopher and reformer John Stuart Mill suddenly fell into a deep two-year depression. In his autobiography, he recounts how it was triggered by a simple question he asked himself:

> "Suppose that all your objects in life were realized; that all the changes in institutions and opinions which you are looking forward to, could be completely effected at this very instant: would this be a great joy and happiness to you?" And an irrepressible self-consciousness distinctly answered, "No!" At this my heart sank within me: the whole foundation on which my life was constructed fell down.

I sometimes ask myself Mill's question, especially when caught up in the maelstrom of American cultural politics. Curiously, Mill finally emerged from his depressive episode by reading the poetry of William Wordsworth. That's not likely to be an antidote these days (though who knows?), for the concomitant question this last year has been, "Will the world as I know it end with the election of Donald J. Trump?" The answer, as usual, is both yes and no. The world will go on, and I will live my life more or less the same, but the world will have been altered. To what extent it's impossible to say, though I would venture that people will die of it. Last summer, Barry Hill asked me what I planned to do if Trump won. All I could think to answer was "resist." In writing this today, I am particularly cognizant of the fact that my letter will be read after the election in November, which is now exactly a month away. There's a whiff of futility in that realisation. Why bother?

Both political parties see this election as fundamentally existential, and the anxiety around it is magnified by the state of the polling. What do all the polls tell us? Nothing we didn't already know: that it will undoubtedly be a close election, thanks to the Electoral College. But then, polls are always retrospective and suspect. They're so often wrong no one fully trusts them, or ought not to. Perhaps it's better to follow two predictive tools that are getting some attention of late. The first, the strange but apparently reliable "keys" that the historian Allan Lichtman devised with a Soviet seismologist, Vladimir Keilis-Borok, simply considers thirteen factors that are either true or false. If at least six of them are "true," you get re-elected. He predicts – or rather insists – Harris will win. The second method is based on daily betting data which reflects what people think will happen. Since these people are putting up real money, they tend to be pragmatic. Tom Miller, a data science professor who designed the system, has an excellent track record, so to speak. However, his forecasts, on the website *The Virtual Tout*, have flipflopped several times, so it's unclear if his method is really an improvement on polling. While both Lichtman's and Miller's approaches may seem far-fetched, it will be interesting to see if they turn out to be correct. Of course, their results could simply be flukes, but such systems do suggest the possibility that professional polling might be superseded in the future, if – for instance – AI developed predictive algorithms so precise that outcomes could be known well in advance. At that point, some might wonder if actual voting was even necessary. Ah, brave new world!

But now, staring down the barrel of the next month, I am reminded of the anecdote about Benjamin Franklin on the last day of the Constitutional Convention in Philadelphia, 17 September 1787, when a Mrs Elizabeth Powell asked him, as he emerged from the final session, "Well, Doctor, have we got a republic or a monarchy?" His reply: "A republic, if you can keep it."

Paul Kane

HIGH
NOON

Response to Correspondence

Don Watson

Others might breeze through, but I find the Quarterly Essay a peculiarly demanding assignment – to write, that is. Whatever rickety notion you begin with, you are as if on a makeshift raft and you must cling to it through the rocks and eddies of doubt and misjudgement all the long way, hoping the thing doesn't fall apart or end up stranded in the weeds. Then, just when you have floated to freedom, you come under fire.*

But this is a welcome salvo, and downright restorative. Far from blowing the raft apart, the generous responses to *High Noon* have built it out and up, and with their wisdom and eloquence even tastefully remodelled it.

David Smith has filled out my skeletal knowledge of Detroit, especially its peculiar "saviour," Dan Gilbert, and pointed to the limits and ambiguities characteristic of such "saviours" everywhere. With much more evidence than I managed to present he also demonstrates how Donald Trump uses the failure and dysfunction of Detroit and cities like it to persuade Americans that their country is going to ruin and only he – genius and strongman – can save it.

Like David Smith, Bruce Wolpe and Emma Shortis have alerted me to the limitations of the essay without sinking it. Bruce connects lying to fascism, a point the Democrats seem determined not to make. Only very recently have they used the "F" word, but from the beginning of the campaign it was open to them to say that democracy cannot exist without a firm basis of truth – not perfect but firm – and that Trump's complete disregard for it suits him not to the United States but to Putin's Russia, or other like autocracies.

The so-called existential nature of this election grips – or oppresses – the more because even when the ballot reveals its secrets, we will not know what follows. If we are persuaded that Harris will win, we still can't be sure that this will mean

* I'm tempted to say it's like *The African Queen*, but one can have too many Hollywood analogies.

a peaceful transfer of power, that Trump and his legions will melt away. If we think Trump will win, should we also think that he will do everything he says he will and plant autocracy in Washington, or just do what's necessary to keep him in the White House and out of jail? Bruce is of course right to say that a civil war like the last one is out of the question, but sporadic organised acts of violence conducted by the country's numerous militias are too easily imagined.

The problem with writing about the United States is like the problem with the country itself. It is too vast and multifarious, its histories too various, opinions and worldviews too much at odds with each other for anyone to say credibly that *this* or *that* is the United States, *this* or *that* is the way the citizens think. This is true of any country, of course, or even of any community, but no other country is even half as large or such an outrageous assortment. No other *democratic* country, at least.

There are a hundred other reasons why an outsider should not try to write about the United States, but that's the big one. Yet it is also the reason why writing about the place is just about impossible to resist. It teems with human variety. It teems with stories. That, I suspect the great storyteller Thomas Keneally would avow, is the attraction of it. The essay was worth writing if only for the whirlwind of his response.

When faith ebbs in the United States, go to the literature, as both Keneally and Paul Kane do; and to the language and the songs. Imagine the world without them. Even where it is empty of people – in the deserts of Utah and the south-west, or the mountains of Colorado – extraordinary tales and seductive songs speak for it. That these millions of American stories add up to one common American adventure is an essential foundation of belief; or, we might say, of the binding mythology.

From the beginning, the United States needed myth. We did not need it in Australia: we had Britain. Britain also did for the other essential items of nationhood that the Americans had to fashion for themselves: a flag, an electrifying anthem or two, volcanic religions, Great Awakenings, some towering figures, and equally towering and sinewy rhetoric, all to bind the Union.

The essential binding, of course, is a perception of common interest. The Union can only exist so long as enough of the people have reason to believe that, on balance, it serves their material or spiritual wellbeing. Millions of Americans will vote for Donald Trump for no better reason than their conviction that gasoline is always dearer when the Democrats are in charge. Millions more will vote for him because they think he is the preferred instrument of God. Yet more will find those two arguments combined are irresistible, and more still will vote for him because of the inexpressible rage they feel about the destruction of their towns and communities and the assault on their status and dignity as (mainly white) Americans.

"Inexpressible" is where Donald Trump comes in – he is the expression of it. He knows how much they hate.

That he has fashioned their many grievances into a coherent – if venomous and wrong-headed – worldview suggests he also appreciates more than the Democrats do how much they love their part of the country, their way of doing and seeing things, their towns and their fellows. Even those people who have recovered from the years of closures and layoffs look at their rusted-out towns and the households on $35,000 a year and, sharing the same sense of betrayal and neglect as the losers, are as open to Trump messages. Social scientists have identified the syndrome and called it "shared fate." There are around 160 large towns and small cities like this in Wisconsin, Michigan and Pennsylvania. They will decide a couple of vital Senate races and might also decide who wins the White House.

The remarkable thing is that the US has for so long managed to project itself abroad and to itself as one indivisible nation, with a common creed and purpose. In the beginning it was, as Thomas Keneally says, an "experimental field," and the Union has only been maintained by a series of compromises, beginning with the original Grand Compromise of 1787. The Electoral College was a double compromise: to satisfy the slaveholding states and to dampen the potential for demagoguery and disorder. As Paul Kane says, it's a "maddening irony" that an institution created as a brake on popular "excess" has given rise to it and made minority rule possible.

"Excess" might be the right word for the times. No country is more given to it than the United States and no American politician has ever so embodied it as has Trump. None perhaps has ever seen so clearly that excess is not a fringe element in the national psyche and experience but a central one. It is the American appetite for excess that he exploits. He is a vulgarian who knows the vulgar reaches of the mind. The entertainment industry deals in excess: Trump has amplified that trend in politics. Racism, xenophobia, ignorance, anti-intellectualism, greed, violence, religious hysteria, conspiracies; he prods all the sore boils of American history and belief, and all the weaknesses they have created in the Union. All the bindings that have managed to hold the Union together he chafes and unravels. He purifies his legions by stirring passive loathing of liberals and Democrats into something virulent while knocking down the icons of conservative restraint and propriety that might lead them astray. This, above all, is why fascism comes to mind.

As I write this, Trump – along with Hulk Hogan and Elon Musk – is addressing a rally in Madison Square Garden, where in 1939 a massive fascist rally was held. There a huge portrait of George Washington was flanked by swastikas. James Carville, the semi-legendary Democrat strategist, has just posted a YouTube video telling Americans that Trump will do what he has said he will do. He believes that, thanks to the money her campaign has and the Democrats' brilliant "ground game," Harris will win. But if Trump wins, he will at once set about creating an autocracy.

In which case, Paul Kane sees no alternative but to resist. Emma Shortis asks what the options will be for Australia if our very best friend and ally opts out of democracy. "Would we do anything differently?" Sadly, I suspect she knows the answer.

But if Paul has any second thoughts, he knows he will be very welcome to take refuge here. Meanwhile, the Australian government might heed the advice of a Democrat adviser to whom I spoke in Kalamazoo and prepare for the arrival of planes full of democratic Americans. Indeed, Australian immigration agents should already be scouring the country for schoolteachers, tradespeople, scientists and all manner of American energy and genius. Not only would they lift our national output, they might also help correct our own less democratic and more servile tendencies.

Don Watson

Paul Kane is professor emeritus at Vassar College in upstate New York and former artistic director of the Mildura Writers Festival. His latest book of poems, *Earth, Air, Water, Fire*, was produced as a CD set by Farpoint Recordings in Dublin. In 2022 he received the Order of Australia.

Thomas Keneally's novels include *The Chant of Jimmie Blacksmith*, *Schindler's List* and *The People's Train*. He has won the Miles Franklin Award, the Booker Prize, the *Los Angeles Times* Prize, the Mondello Prize and has been made a Literary Lion of the New York Public Library, a Fellow of the American Academy and is a recipient of the University of California gold medal.

George Megalogenis's book *The Australian Moment* won the 2013 Prime Minister's Literary Award for Non-fiction and the 2012 Walkley Award for Non-fiction. He is also author of *Faultlines*, *The Longest Decade*, *Australia's Second Chance*, *The Football Solution* and three previous Quarterly Essays.

Emma Shortis is a senior researcher at the Australia Institute and the author of *Our Exceptional Friend: Australia's fatal alliance with the United States.*

David Smith is an associate professor at the University of Sydney. He has a PhD in political science from the University of Michigan and is the author of *Religious Persecution and Political Order in the United States.*

Don Watson is the author of three Quarterly Essays and many acclaimed books, including *Caledonia Australis*, *Recollections of a Bleeding Heart*, *American Journeys*, *The Bush*, *Watsonia*, *The Story of Australia* and *The Passion of Private White.*

Bruce Wolpe is (non-resident) senior fellow at the United States Studies Centre and the author of *Trump's Australia*. He worked with the Democrats in the US Congress during President Barack Obama's first term.

QUARTERLY ESSAY BACK ISSUES

- ☐ **QE 1** *In Denial* by Robert Manne $27.99
- ☐ **QE 2** *Appeasing Jakarta* by John Birmingham $27.99
- ☐ **QE 3** *The Opportunist* by Guy Rundle $27.99
- ☐ **QE 4** *Rabbit Syndrome* by Don Watson $27.99
- ☐ **QE 5** *Girt By Sea* by Mungo MacCallum $27.99
- ☐ **QE 6** *Beyond Belief* by John Button $27.99
- ☐ **QE 7** *Paradise Betrayed* by John Martinkus $27.99
- **QE 8** *Groundswell* by Amanda Lohrey OUT OF STOCK
- ☐ **QE 9** *Beautiful Lies* by Tim Flannery $27.99
- ☐ **QE 10** *Bad Company* by Gideon Haigh $27.99
- ☐ **QE 11** *Whitefella Jump Up* by Germaine Greer $27.99
- ☐ **QE 12** *Made in England* by David Malouf $27.99
- ☐ **QE 13** *Sending Them Home* by Robert Manne with David Corlett $27.99
- ☐ **QE 14** *Mission Impossible* by Paul McGeough $27.99
- ☐ **QE 15** *Latham's World* by Margaret Simons $27.99
- ☐ **QE 16** *Breach of Trust* by Raimond Gaita $27.99
- ☐ **QE 17** *'Kangaroo Court'* by John Hirst $27.99
- ☐ **QE 18** *The Worried Well* by Gail Bell $27.99
- ☐ **QE 19** *Relaxed & Comfortable* by Judith Brett $27.99
- ☐ **QE 20** *A Time for War* by John Birmingham $27.99
- ☐ **QE 21** *What's Left? by Clive Hamilton* $27.99
- ☐ **QE 22** *Voting for Jesus* by Amanda Lohrey $27.99
- ☐ **QE 23** *The History Question* by Inga Clendinnen $27.99
- ☐ **QE 24** *No Fixed Address* by Robyn Davidson $27.99
- ☐ **QE 25** *Bipolar Nation* by Peter Hartcher $27.99
- ☐ **QE 26** *His Master's Voice* by David Marr $27.99
- ☐ **QE 27** *Reaction Time* by Ian Lowe $27.99
- ☐ **QE 28** *Exit Right* by Judith Brett $27.99
- ☐ **QE 29** *Love & Money* by Anne Manne $27.99
- ☐ **QE 30** *Last Drinks* by Paul Toohey $27.99
- ☐ **QE 31** *Now or Never* by Tim Flannery $27.99
- ☐ **QE 32** *American Revolution* by Kate Jennings $27.99
- ☐ **QE 33** *Quarry Vision* by Guy Pearse $27.99
- ☐ **QE 34** *Stop at Nothing* by Annabel Crabb $27.99
- ☐ **QE 35** *Radical Hope* by Noel Pearson $27.99
- ☐ **QE 36** *Australian Story* by Mungo MacCallum $27.99
- ☐ **QE 37** *What's Right?* by Waleed Aly $27.99
- ☐ **QE 38** *Power Trip* by David Marr $27.99
- ☐ **QE 39** *Power Shift* by Hugh White $27.99
- ☐ **QE 40** *Trivial Pursuit* by George Megalogenis $27.99
- ☐ **QE 41** *The Happy Life* by David Malouf $27.99
- ☐ **QE 42** *Fair Share* by Judith Brett $27.99
- ☐ **QE 43** *Bad News* by Robert Manne $27.99
- ☐ **QE 44** *Man-Made World* by Andrew Charlton $27.99
- ☐ **QE 45** *Us and Them* by Anna Krien $27.99
- ☐ **QE 46** *Great Expectations* by Laura Tingle $27.99
- ☐ **QE 47** *Political Animal* by David Marr $27.99
- ☐ **QE 48** *After the Future* by Tim Flannery $27.99
- ☐ **QE 49** *Not Dead Yet* by Mark Latham $27.99
- ☐ **QE 50** *Unfinished Business* by Anna Goldsworthy $27.99
- ☐ **QE 51** *The Prince* by David Marr $27.99
- ☐ **QE 52** *Found in Translation* by Linda Jaivin $27.99
- ☐ **QE 53** *That Sinking Feeling* by Paul Toohey $27.99
- ☐ **QE 54** *Dragon's Tail* by Andrew Charlton $27.99
- ☐ **QE 55** *A Rightful Place* by Noel Pearson $27.99
- ☐ **QE 56** *Clivosaurus* by Guy Rundle $27.99
- ☐ **QE 57** *Dear Life* by Karen Hitchcock $27.99
- ☐ **QE 58** *Blood Year* by David Kilcullen $27.99
- ☐ **QE 59** *Faction Man* by David Marr $27.99
- ☐ **QE 60** *Political Amnesia* by Laura Tingle $27.99
- ☐ **QE 61** *Balancing Act* by George Megalogenis $27.99
- ☐ **QE 62** *Firing Line* by James Brown $27.99
- ☐ **QE 63** *Enemy Within* by Don Watson $27.99
- ☐ **QE 64** *The Australian Dream* by Stan Grant $27.99
- ☐ **QE 65** *The White Queen* by David Marr $27.99
- ☐ **QE 66** *The Long Goodbye* by Anna Krien $27.99
- ☐ **QE 67** *Moral Panic 101* by Benjamin Law $27.99
- ☐ **QE 68** *Without America* by Hugh White $27.99

QUARTERLY ESSAY BACK ISSUES

- ☐ **QE 69** *Moment of Truth* by Mark McKenna $27.99
- ☐ **QE 70** *Dead Right* by Richard Denniss $27.99
- ☐ **QE 71** *Follow the Leader* by Laura Tingle $27.99
- ☐ **QE 72** *Net Loss* by Sebastian Smee $27.99
- ☐ **QE 73** *Australia Fair* by Rebecca Huntley $27.99
- ☐ **QE 74** *The Prosperity Gospel* by Erik Jensen $27.99
- ☐ **QE 75** *Men at Work* by Annabel Crabb $27.99
- ☐ **QE 76** *Red Flag* by Peter Hartcher $27.99
- ☐ **QE 77** *Cry Me a River* by Margaret Simons $27.99
- ☐ **QE 78** *The Coal Curse* by Judith Brett $27.99
- ☐ **QE 79** *The End of Certainty* by Katharine Murphy $27.99
- ☐ **QE 80** *The High Road* by Laura Tingle $27.99
- ☐ **QE 81** *Getting to Zero* by Alan Finkel $27.99
- ☐ **QE 82** *Exit Strategy* by George Megalogenis $27.99
- ☐ **QE 83** *Top Blokes* by Lech Blaine $27.99
- ☐ **QE 84** *The Reckoning* by Jess Hill $27.99
- ☐ **QE 85** *Not Waving, Drowning* by Sarah Krasnostein $27.99
- ☐ **QE 86** *Sleepwalk to War* by Hugh White $27.99
- ☐ **QE 87** *Uncivil Wars* by Waleed Aly & Scott Stephens $27.99
- ☐ **QE 88** *Lone Wolf* by Katharine Murphy $27.99
- ☐ **QE 89** *The Wires That Bind* by Saul Griffith $27.99
- ☐ **QE 90** *Voice of Reason* by Megan Davis $27.99
- ☐ **QE 91** *Lifeboat* by Micheline Lee $27.99
- ☐ **QE 92** *The Great Divide* by Alan Kohler $27.99
- ☐ **QE 93** *Bad Cop* by Lech Blaine $27.99
- ☐ **QE 94** *Highway to Hell* by Joëlle Gergis $27.99
- ☐ **QE 95** *High Noon* by Don Watson $27.99

Order back issues online

Prices include GST.
$10 flat-rate shipping within Australia.
Please include this form with delivery and payment details overleaf.
Back issues also available as ebooks from ebook retailers.